MANAGEMENT
Sixth Edition

Principles and Practices

Paul B. Thornton

Kendall Hunt
publishing company

Cover image © Shutterstock.com

Kendall Hunt
publishing company

www.kendallhunt.com
Send all inquiries to:
4050 Westmark Drive
Dubuque, IA 52004-1840

Copyright © 2017 by Kendall Hunt Publishing Company

ISBN: 978-1-5249-3286-2

Published in the United States of America

Dedicated to

Elizabeth Justine Bernadette Thornton—

My mother gave me unconditional love, support,
and encouragement.

CONTENTS

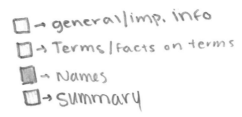

☐ → general/imp. info
☐ → Terms/facts on terms
■ → Names
▣ → Summary

Acknowledgments   vii

Introduction   ix

PART I—The Basics   1

CHAPTER 1   Management Defined 3

PART II—The Context   11

CHAPTER 2   The Context 13
CHAPTER 3   Mission, Vision, and Values 21
CHAPTER 4   Business Strategy 29
CHAPTER 5   Organizational Structure 37

PART III—The Manager   47

CHAPTER 6   Core Beliefs and Behavior 49
CHAPTER 7   Management Styles 53
CHAPTER 8   Power and Influence 59
CHAPTER 9   Approaches to Leading Others 65

PART IV—The Process   71

CHAPTER 10   Managing the Process 73
CHAPTER 11   Managing Performance 79
CHAPTER 12   Creating, Managing, and Leading Teams 89

PART V—Management Skills   99

CHAPTER 13   Managing Time 101
CHAPTER 14   Sending and Receiving Messages 109
CHAPTER 15   Making Presentations 115
CHAPTER 16   Writing Messages 119

CHAPTER 17 Conducting Interviews 125

CHAPTER 18 Conducting Meetings 133

CHAPTER 19 Solving Problems 139

CHAPTER 20 Resolving Conflicts 147

CHAPTER 21 Motivating Others 157

CHAPTER 22 Managing Stress 163

CHAPTER 23 Dealing with Difficult People 169

CHAPTER 24 Managing Your Career 177

Research   **185**

About the Author   **187**

ACKNOWLEDGMENTS

Most of the theories in this book are long-standing. I am greatly indebted to those who have educated me (especially Dr. Paul Hersey) in these management and leadership concepts.

Special thanks to the following people:

My wife, Mary Jean, who is a seasoned executive and leader. She has taught management courses at Capital Community College for the past twelve years. Over the past twenty years we have discussed just about every management topic in this book.

- Paul Bureau, Kate Labor, and Andrew Thornton for reading various chapters and providing valuable feedback.
- Bridget Finn for typing and proofreading sections of my manuscript.
- Michael Dowling provided great advice and guidance in helping with the design and layout of several chapters.
- My students at STCC and numerous participants in seminars and workshops who have shared their insights and ideas about what both the best managers and the worst managers do.
- Finally, I would like to thank Amanda Smith, Karen Fleckenstein, and the Kendall Hunt Publishing team for the cover design, layout, and editing of my complete manuscript. They did an outstanding job.

INTRODUCTION

Welcome!

I began playing organized hockey when I was twelve. By the time I entered Canton High School as a freshman, I had become good enough to make the varsity team. I was always curious to know why some teams in my league consistently excelled (unfortunately, that didn't include my team) and others floundered. Summoning all of my teenage wisdom, I concluded that the difference was due to coaching, and I began studying what the top coaches did to bring out the best in each player and their teams. This sparked my lifelong interest in management and leadership.

While a student at Ohio University, I took a terrific course taught by a terrific teacher: Managing Organizational Behavior by Dr. Paul Hersey. His knowledge and passion for the subject further ignited my interest in management and leadership. After graduating, no NHL teams were clamoring for my services. I worked a few years in sales but that wasn't my passion. At age 27, I accepted a teaching and coaching position (varsity hockey) at American International College. This experience gave me the opportunity to apply some of the concepts and theories I learned in college. But I quickly realized theory is one thing; applying it in the real world is something else.

Over the past thirty years I have observed, studied, and interviewed hundreds of the top business managers and leaders to identify what they do to bring out the best in their people. This book describes the core principles and practices that the best managers use to be both efficient and effective.

Part I

THE BASICS

What do managers do?

What types of resources do they have to get the job done?

What is the difference between being effective and being efficient?

Should managers focus more on the task or the people?

What about customers? Where do they fit into the equation?

What does it mean to manage your boss?

Chapter 1 is my attempt to answer some of these basic questions about management. To begin, it's important to have a clear and understandable definition of the word "management."

Having the title of *manager* is a <u>great</u> responsibility! Your actions have an impact on people's lives, your business, and the community in which you operate.

Chapter 1

MANAGEMENT DEFINED

Peter is a sales manager. Rhoda is a finance manager. Kate is a general manager.

What is the common theme that runs through all of their jobs? They are all managers and all managers work with and through people to accomplish specific goals.

There are many different definitions of leadership. Mine is very simple and straightforward.

Management is the process of working with and through people to achieve organizational goals.

Managers have five basic resources to get the job done.

1. **Human resources** are people. Managers are responsible for hiring, training, and motivating employees. Entrepreneur and business leader Mary Kay Ash said, "People are definitely a company's greatest asset. It doesn't make any difference whether the product is cars or cosmetics. A company is only as good as the people it keeps."

2. **Financial resources** refer to money and budgets. Most managers have a budget to operate their area or department. Managers must achieve goals while operating within the allowed budget.

3. **Physical resources** refer to the machines, materials, and equipment needed to produce products and services. Of course, the physical resources will vary depending on the type of products and services your company produces and the function you are in.

4. **Information**—Managers acquire and utilize information about people (employees and customers), products, competitors, and economic trends. They use information to identify problems and opportunities and evaluate options.

5. **Time** is a limited resource. Managers must spend their time focused on the right things. New managers quickly discover that setting priorities and managing their time is a critical skill.

EFFICIENT AND EFFECTIVE

The best managers are both efficient and effective in using their resources.

▶ Being <u>efficient</u> means "no waste." Waste produces unnecessary costs. All five resources need to be used in the most productive way.

▶ Being <u>effective</u> refers to being focused on the right things. An effective manager has the right priorities and is focused on the right goals. Peter F. Drucker, the father of modern-day management said, "Efficiency is doing the thing right. Effectiveness is doing the right thing."

Efficient but ineffective—Some managers are very efficient. They use their resources in the most productive ways. But they are focused on the wrong goals and priorities. Former author and consultant Stephen Covey once said, "If the ladder is not leaning against the right wall, every step we take just gets us to the wrong place faster."

Effective but inefficient—On the other hand, some managers are focused on the right goals, but they are very inefficient and wasteful in using their resources.

In today's business environment, managers are given fewer resources but expected to get more done in less time. The pressure is on to be lean and highly efficient. Managers are required to eliminate every bit of waste in every process.

LEVELS OF MANAGEMENT

Depending on the size of the company, there are various levels of management.

▶ **Senior Management** refers to the president and vice presidents. They are responsible for strategic planning, building the culture, managing the middle managers, and the organization's overall performance. Ultimately they are responsible for profit and loss.

▶ **Middle Managers** refers to the directors and managers who are responsible for allocating resources, implementing plans, monitoring progress, and managing the first-line managers.

▶ **First-Line Managers** are responsible for the day-to-day management of the employees who are doing the work to produce the products and services that are provided to the external and internal customers.

TASK AND PEOPLE

All managers must focus on both the <u>task</u>—the work to be done—and the <u>relationships</u> they have with the people who are doing the work.

Task-oriented behaviors include the following:

▶ Defining the task or problem
▶ Discussing options
▶ Clarifying goals

- ▶ Assigning roles and responsibilities
- ▶ Establishing deadlines
- ▶ Monitoring and measuring results

F. W. Taylor, the originator of the Scientific Management movement, focused on the task. His goal was to improve the productivity and efficiency of manual workers. He used the scientific method to discover the "one best way" to do a task. His "time and motion" studies were used to identify the best techniques to increase productivity.

In some ways, it makes sense to think of management as a science that focuses on the most efficient way to get the task done. Certainly using data to measure, analyze, and evaluate performance is useful. But it is equally important for managers to build good relationships with the people they are working with.

People-oriented behaviors include the following:

- ▶ Listening
- ▶ Encouraging
- ▶ Including
- ▶ Supporting
- ▶ Harmonizing
- ▶ Giving recognition

The best managers have good interpersonal skills—good people skills. They relate well to people and connect in positive ways.

In the 1920s and early 1930s, the task focused/Scientific Management emphasis started by Taylor was replaced by the Human Relations Movement, initiated by Elton Mayo and his associates. They believed the real power centers in organizations were the interpersonal relations that developed within the working unit. According to the Human Relations Movement, human interactions are the most important consideration for a manager.

In essence then, the scientific management movement emphasized a concern for task (output) while the human relations movement stressed a concern for relationships (people).

- ▶ *Overly task focused*—Some managers are too task-focused. For example, Ralph manages a group of seven people. He is all about the work that needs to be done. He never makes small talk or reaches out to people as people. For him, the only thing that matters is results. Duke basketball coach Mike Krzyzewski once said, "A common mistake among those who work in sport is spending a disproportionate amount of time on 'x's and o's' as compared to time spent learning about people."
- ▶ *Overly people focused*—On the other hand some managers are too people-focused. They have a big need to be liked by everyone. They bend the rules and don't hold employees accountable for completing assignments. They go overboard trying to make people happy and create harmony among them. These managers avoid conflict and usually accommodate employees even when it sets a bad precedent.

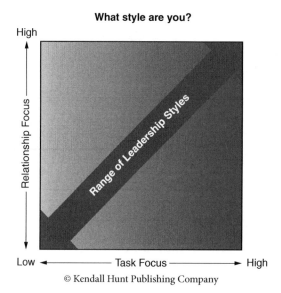

© Kendall Hunt Publishing Company

Most managers gravitate to one or the other: task or people. The best managers maintain a good balance and focus on both the work to be done <u>and</u> the people doing it. Certainly, different situations may require managers to spend more time on the task side or the people side of the equation. In a crisis situation, managers need to be more focused on the task (put the fire out) than on building relationships.

> During the summer of 2011, my mother had an operation for lung cancer. During her seven-day hospital stay I had an opportunity to observe several doctors and nurses. Some of the doctors and nurses were all about the task. They could explain procedures, medications, and next steps, etc., but they lacked people skills. However, one doctor and one nurse stood out. They were not only very good technically but also had great people skills. Figure out what you do naturally and then develop reminders and checklists to help you learn to do the other equally well.

THE MANAGER'S RESPONSIBILITIES

Managers must manage up, laterally, and down.

Dee Hock, former CEO of Visa, describes the key responsibilities of managers this way:

1. **The first responsibility** of anyone that manages is to manage themselves. Managers set the example for their group. If you can't manage yourself, how can you manage others?

2. **The second responsibility** is to manage your boss. Bosses determine the resources managers get to do their job, so it is important to build a strong working relationship with your boss. Know what is most important to your boss and make sure those priorities are met.

3. **The third responsibility** is to manage your peers. Building relationships with peers is important because they are often the internal customers and suppliers to the manager's group. In addition, they provide information, support, and help managers achieve their goals.

4. **The fourth responsibility** is to manage your direct reports. The best managers train and motivate their employees to perform at their best. The former CEO of Southwest Airlines, Herb Kelleher, once said, "When we focus on the employee experience, the employee will focus on the customer experience, when customers are happy they come back which makes the shareholders happy and ultimately increases shareholder value."

The job of a manager is broader than just managing your direct reports. Successful managers understand the importance of building and strengthening relationships with their boss and peers.

It is important to note that it all starts with setting a good example. In the role of manager, you are a role model. All eyes are on you. The example you set has an enormous impact on your direct reports, and those around you. Some of the things you can do to set a good example include:

- Always be on time and prepared
- Follow through on commitments
- Be a good listener
- Collaborate and be open to new ideas
- Treat everyone with respect
- Tell the truth—be a straight shooter

SUMMARY

The important things you, the manager, need to remember . . .

- Efficiently and effectively use your resources to meet and exceed customer expectations.
- Have an appropriate balance between being "task focused" and "people focused."
- Manage up (your boss), laterally (your peers), and down (your employees).
- Set a good example.

DISCUSSION QUESTIONS

1. Is it better to be efficient or effective?

2. Assume you have been hired as a new customer service manager at L.L. Bean. Ten people report to you. They take orders over the phone and Internet. In addition, they answer questions and resolve customer complaints. Describe the top five actions you will take during your first week on the job.

3. In making the transition to manager, how would you go about establishing a manager-employee relationship with a personal friend?

4. Complete the "Management Style" exercise to determine your task score and your relationship score.

MANAGEMENT STYLE EXERCISE

Assignment: Assume you are a team leader. Circle the choice that best applies to your leadership approach.

Always	Frequently	Sometimes	Seldom	Never
A	B	C	D	E

A B C D E   1. I try to know the names of each team member's spouse and children.

A B C D E   2. I give my team members encouragement and emotional support.

A B C D E   3. A productive team needs a delicate balance of skills and personality.

A B C D E   4. I give praise to or express appreciation for my team members.

A B C D E   5. I try to select team members whose personalities will blend well.

A B C D E   6. I try to include all team members in discussions.

A B C D E   7. I work to build team spirit.

A B C D E   8. I enjoy building positive relationships with other team members.

A B C D E   9. I find things to like in each of my team members.

A B C D E   10. I try to help team members manage conflicts.

A B C D E   11. I assign specific roles and responsibilities to each team member.

A B C D E   12. I know how much each team member is accomplishing.

A B C D E   13. I discourage discussion of personal issues during working hours.

A B C D E   14. I encourage work after hours to complete a project.

A B C D E   15. My team members know exactly what is expected of them.

A B C D E   16. Projects progress on a predictable schedule.

A B C D E   17. I set deadlines for the completion of assigned tasks.

A B C D E   18. When I reward and recognize employees, I focus on the work they did.

A B C D E   19. I establish tight controls, assuring the task is completed on schedule.

A B C D E   20. My major focus is completing the task on time and within budget.

Turn Page for Scoring and Interpreting

Scoring

A) For each item, convert what you circled to the following:

Always	+2
Frequently	+1
Sometimes	0
Seldom	−1
Never	−2

B) Add up items 1–10. That's your relationship score.

C) Add up items 11–20. That's your task score.

Interpreting Your Scores

A high relationship score means that you are more people-oriented. A high task score means that you are more task-focused. To be a good manager, you want to create a balanced score.

Part II

THE CONTEXT

What is going on in the marketplace?

What are the company's mission, vision, and values?

How does the company make money?

What do the company's financials indicate?

What is the company culture?

What is the company's strategy and structure?

What is important to know about the formal and informal organizational structure?

Chapters 2 through 5 answer these questions. It's crucial to understand the environment or context in which you are managing. There are major differences between hospitals, manufacturing companies, colleges and universities, retail stores, and not-for-profit organizations.

All logos/© Shutterstock.com

Chapter 2

THE CONTEXT

Is being a manager at McDonald's the same as being a manager at Google?

What do managers need to know about the environment they are in?

There are a number of things that managers need to understand about the environment they are in. These include the general business context, financial context, and the company culture.

THE GENERAL BUSINESS ENVIRONMENT

Managers operate in a challenging, demanding, and uncertain world. At some point, every manager will face some of the following challenges:

- ▶ Customers want more quality, more options, better service, and lower prices.
- ▶ Bosses require managers to get more done, faster, and with fewer resources.
- ▶ Employees want pay increases, better benefits, up-to-date training, and opportunities for advancement.
- ▶ Stockholders want bigger dividends and increases in stock value.
- ▶ The competition keeps improving. They are doing everything they can to entice your customers to buy from them.
- ▶ Technological advances increase the pressure to keep learning and stay up-to-date.

Managers must walk a fine line and satisfy groups that often have contradictory and competing interests. For example, customers want lower prices and employees want higher pay and increased benefits. Today's business world is filled with many challenges which requires managers to be highly efficient and effective in everything they do.

THE FINANCIAL CONTEXT

Managers operate within a financial environment that involves budgets, expenses, balance sheets, and income statements.

An **income statement** is a report that shows how much revenue a company earned over a specific time period. It also shows the costs and expenses associated with earning that revenue. The literal "bottom line" of the statement usually shows the company's net earnings or losses. To simplify managers need to understand this simple formula:

$$\text{REVENUE} - \text{EXPENSES} = \text{PROFIT}$$

Revenue

Selling your products and services brings money into your business. Companies try to increase sales in one or more of the following ways:

- ▶ Increase sales of current products to current customers.
- ▶ Increase their customer base.
- ▶ Develop new products and services for current and/or new customers.

Growth in your top line from sales shows that customers are valuing your products. Chris Manolakis, the President of Abbett Business Services, Inc. said, "One way to increase sales is through co-branding. If you run a gas station or convenience store, consider leasing out space for a Dunkin Donuts or Subway operation. This can be a win-win deal."

In general, companies are doing whatever they can to increase sales and revenue.

Expenses

Think of expenses as what it costs to produce and sell your products and services. In general, companies want to increase revenue and reduce expenses. Bob Fifer, author of *Double Your Profit*, said that there are two types of costs:

- ▶ *Strategic costs*—everything done to bring in new business, such as advertising, sales reps, and promotional programs.
- ▶ *Non-strategic costs*—the costs of running the business, such as rent, utilities, and office supplies.

Fifer's philosophy is that while you should spend more than the competition on strategic costs, you don't waste money; you need to spend it on the "right things." Aggressively cut non-strategic costs to the bone. In addition, managers can reduce costs by simplifying processes and eliminating waste. Managers should always be trying to increase efficiency.

Profit

It's the famous "bottom line"! Add up your revenue and subtract expenses; what remains is profit. Profit is good—the more the better. Profitable companies have money to reward employees and stockholders, invest in new technology, and develop new products.

Managers need to understand the big financial picture. Specifically, they need to understand what's happening with revenues, expenses, and profit. The best managers have a solid understanding of the metrics their company uses to track each of these variables. In addition, it is important to understand both the current numbers and the trends. Here are some common situations that happen at some companies.

- ► Sales increase but expenses rise faster resulting in smaller profit margins
- ► Sales take a dramatic downturn but management fails to take decisive action to reduce expenses which causes larger losses
- ► Sales are flat but expenses keep increasing

ORGANIZATIONAL CULTURE

Just as individuals have personalities, so, too, do organizations. Organizational culture is a company's personality. It's based on a set of shared beliefs and values. Culture guides employees on how they should think and behave. It defines the norms and standards of desired behavior. Tony Hsieh, CEO of Zappos once said, "At Zappos, we view culture as our number-one priority. We decided that if we get the culture right, most of the stuff, like building a brand around delivering the very best customer service, will just take care of itself."

A strong company culture is one in which a large percentage of the managers and employees share the same values and beliefs. A strong culture sends a clear and powerful message as to what's important and what the organization stands for. Managers and leaders practice what they preach. Their words and actions align with the company's core beliefs and values.

To understand the company culture it's helpful to consider the following:

- ► Who gets promoted?
- ► What behaviors get rewarded?
- ► What slogans and stories are heard most often?
- ► What is the compensation system based on?
- ► Does the physical environment indicate what is important?
- ► What are the company rituals?

The answers to these questions provides insight as to what a company really values and believes in.

Some of the most common types of cultures include the following:

Bureaucratic Culture

The government and correctional institutions are good examples of bureaucratic cultures. They have lots of rules, regulations, and procedures. Bureaucratic cultures are dull, slow moving, and risk adverse. When problems occur, administrators create new rules and procedures. The chain of command is followed religiously and seniority is an important factor in promotions.

Entrepreneurial Culture

The entrepreneurial culture is perhaps the opposite of the bureaucratic culture. This culture has few rules and procedures. It values creativity and risk taking (breaking the rules) to take advantage of opportunities. Entrepreneurial cultures are prepared to identify and act on new ideas quickly. They learn from their mistakes and keep experimenting with their ideas and product offerings.

Service Culture

Companies with a strong service culture often provide customers with experiences that are unique and memorable. Providing service that meets or exceeds customers' expectations is the norm. These cultures are "customer centric." All decisions are made with "wowing the customer" as the most important criteria.

> A few years ago my wife and I went on vacation and stayed at The Breakers Hotel in Palm Beach Florida. Several days prior to our arrival I received the following e-mail. "You are about to enjoy a stay that will exceed your every expectation." I must say, they lived up to their high standards.

Family Culture

The family culture treats all employees as part of the family. Loyalty and nepotism are characteristics of a family culture. A family culture tends to be a more forgiving environment. Employees who aren't meeting expectations are given second and third chances. You can't fire a family member. But no matter how talented and great a performer you are the next vice president is going to be the owner's son or daughter. Family cultures can place great demands on direct family members. For example, the owner's son or daughter–in-law may be expected to work 12-hour days or all weekends if necessary to get the job done.

Performance Culture

Steve Jobs once stated, "Some people aren't used to an environment where excellence is expected." These cultures most value great performance or improved results. It doesn't matter who you know or what credentials you possess, what matters is your performance. Hitting your targets is the standard by which all employees are judged. Continuous improvement is also an important aspect of these cultures.

Norman Love, Founder and CEO, Norman Love Confections

Norman states, "The best leadership advice I received came from Mr. Horst Schulte, former CEO of the Ritz-Carlton Company. He told me long ago to go to work with a purpose, to go to work striving to be excellent every day. In fact, to go to work to be better than you were yesterday. This is our philosophy, my employees and I, and has been since day one."

Managers need to understand the company's culture. This helps them to set goals, make decisions, and focus on what's most important.

MANAGING IN A DEMANDING ENVIRONMENT

Managers must be effective and efficient. They must be crystal clear on their goals and priorities. In addition, they must utilize their resources in the most productive way possible.

Therefore, managers also need ***to be leaders***. What's the difference between managing and leading?

- ▶ **Managers** use current methods, procedures, and resources to get the job done.
- ▶ **Leaders** focus on change. Leaders have ideas and visions about how to improve the status quo. They want to change things for the better.

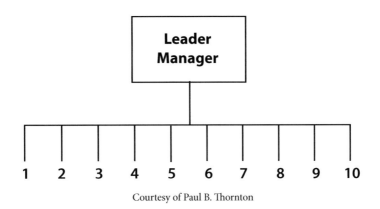

Courtesy of Paul B. Thornton

The former president of Management Development International, Mike Gabi, once said,

"I'd like to create a new word that combines both roles—manager and leader. In a 30-minute meeting, I may spend 10 minutes managing and 20 minutes leading. Both sets of skills are critical for all managers."

Dr. John C. Maxwell, author of numerous books on leadership, maintains there is always a better, simpler, faster, more efficient, more creative way to get the job done. Managers must embrace and practice the "R" words:

- ► Reinvent
- ► Reimagine
- ► Reengineer
- ► Redesign

This requires managers to be open, curious, and committed to life-long learning. The learning cycle includes three steps—finding new ideas, experimenting, and fine-tuning.

Finding New Ideas

How do managers and leaders discover new ideas?

1. Ask lots of questions.
2. Read articles and books.
3. Interview experts.
4. Observe best practices.
5. Brainstorm.
6. Talk to people in different fields.
7. Attend seminars and conferences.

Experimenting

Ideas are important, but they must be tested. Hugely successful former Tennessee women's basketball coach Pat Summit said, "The willingness to experiment with change may be the most essential ingredient to success at anything." Does the idea hold up in practice? You need to test your ideas by doing experiments, pilot programs, and getting feedback from focus groups.

Fine-Tune

Just as a musician fine-tunes his instrument, managers need to fine-tune their ideas. Keep making small changes to achieve the desired goal.

The best managers are committed to life-long improvement. They know survival depends on finding new, more efficient ways to meet and exceed customer expectations.

SUMMARY

The one thing you need to remember . . .

Managers must have a solid understanding of the context or environment they are operating in.

DISCUSSION QUESTIONS

1. What are the differences between "worry" and "reflection"?

2. How much time should managers spend in the role of "managing" versus "leading"?

3. How would you describe the culture of the family you grew up in?

4. You have just been hired as a management trainee for a manufacturing company. It's your first day! You will meet with your boss that afternoon. She said that you should send her an e-mail with some of your questions so that she can be better prepared for the meeting. What are the top three questions that you will want to discuss?

Chapter 3

MISSION, VISION, AND VALUES

What is the foundation of every great business?

What is the mission of every manager?

The foundation of a company is its mission, vision, and values. Company leaders must provide simple, clear, and compelling answers to these three questions:

1. What's our mission or purpose?

2. What's our vision or long-term goals?

3. What are our values or guiding principles?

Without mission, there's no purpose. Without vision, there's no destination. Without values, there are no guiding principles. When the mission, vision, and values are clear, it creates a framework to set goals, evaluate options, and make decisions.

MISSION

A company's mission is its purpose or reason for being. An effective mission statement provides managers and employees with focus, inspiration, and criteria to evaluate strategic choices. Howard Schultz, CEO of Starbucks, once said, "People want to be part of something larger than themselves. They want to be part of something they're really proud of, that they'll fight for, sacrifice for, that they trust."

The way a company states its mission has a direct impact on the focus of employees and the initiatives it pursues. Here is an example:

Airline A: "Our *mission is to transport people from one location to another.*"

Airline B: "Our *mission is to entertain people at 25,000 feet.*"

At Airline A, employees are focused and inspired to efficiently transport people. At Airline B, employees are focused on entertaining passengers as they fly to their destination. *"What types of movies, music, and drinks can we provide to make the trip enjoyable? What experiences can we provide to make the trip memorable?"*

Ineffective Mission Statements

Some company's mission statements miss the mark for a variety of reasons.

▶ **Too narrow:** Companies that said their mission was "to make buggy whips" no longer exist. As times changed, they became obsolete. In a *Harvard Business Review* article, Theodore Levitt wrote that the railroad industry caused its own decline by insisting that "*We're in the railroad business.*" If they had said, "We're in the transportation business," they could have expanded into trucks, buses, and airlines.

▶ **Too long:** Mission statements that are long, drawn out, rambling statements aren't read, let alone remembered. I have read some mission statements that were over 120 words long. I got lost in the minutia. Business leaders should be able to state their mission in twenty words or less.

▶ **Gobbledygook:** Some mission statements are packed full of jargon and vague terms which makes them uninspiring and hard to understand.

> "Our mission is to develop, deploy, and manage a diverse set of six sigma quality and strategic knowledge management tools to best serve our constituents, partners, and collaborative organizations, improving the possibility of overall satisfaction among diverse customer profiles."

Huh? What does all that mean? It lacks clarity. It's not inspiring.

Effective Mission Statements

An effective mission statement captures an organization's unique and enduring reason for being. They align and focus employees in a common direction. Here are several examples of effective mission statements.

1. **Google:** "To organize the world's information and make it universally accessible and useful."

2. **Lowe's:** "Helping customers build, improve and enjoy their homes."

3. **Ben & Jerry's:** "To make, distribute, and sell the finest quality, all-natural ice cream and related products in a wide variety of innovative flavors made from Vermont dairy products."

4. **Merck:** "To preserve and improve human life."

5. **Starbucks:** "To inspire and nurture the human spirit—one person, one cup, and one neighborhood at a time."

Developing a simple and clear mission statement takes thoughtful reflection and many rewrites. Every mission statement, no matter how large or successful the organization, needs to be reviewed annually to test its relevance in the current environment. Like a good foundation, it doesn't have to be fancy, but it must be solid.

VISION

Theodore Hesburgh, former President, University of Notre Dame, once said, "The very essence of leadership is that you have to have a vision. It's got to be a vision you articulate clearly and forcefully on every occasion." A vision statement is an aspirational statement. It describes a future that's better in some important way, compared to what currently exists. It is the desired end-state.

Vision implies you can see it. The challenge for managers and leaders is communicating an image of the future that draws people in. You want people to see it, believe it, and be inspired to pursue it. A compelling vision keeps people energized and motivated as they work day-to-day.

Dave Logan, President, Palmer Foundry states, "I look at vision as the dream we all need. Dreams are what make life exciting and interesting. During the past year, our business suffered a catastrophic loss due to a massive fire. Much of the plant was destroyed. Everything looked like a mess, felt like a mess, and it was very difficult to see beyond the rubble.

We needed a vision. We needed a positive picture of the future to buoy our spirits as we argued with the insurance company, dealt with concerned customers, and slowly rebuilt our business. We faced many investment decisions as we rebuilt. Knowing what type of product we wanted to make and the type of customer we wanted to serve guided us during the reconstruction process. With so many decisions to make, having a focused vision kept our team pulling in the same direction.

Ineffective Vision Statements

Here are some reasons why some vision statements are ineffective.

- ▶ **Too long:** Some vision statements are simply too long and unclear. It takes some leaders three paragraphs or 300 words to explain where they want to get to. Leaders should be able to describe their vision in twenty-five words or less.

- ▶ **Too general:** Some companies have vision statements that could pass for just about any company in their industry. If your vision is too general, it doesn't excite and engage people.

- ▶ **Too abstract:** Visions are meant to be seen. Employees need to be able to form a clear, concrete picture in their mind as to where the company is headed.

- ▶ **Too much gobblegook:** Drop the buzzwords and jargon. They're confusing and uninspiring. A vision needs to be easy to understand for all employees from the CEO to the hourly employees.

Effective Vision Statements

Some examples of effective vision statements include:

1. **President John F. Kennedy:** "Land a man on the moon and safely return him to Earth by the end of this decade."

2. **Microsoft Corporation:** The original version was "A computer on every desk and in every home."

3. **Alzheimer's Association:** "Our vision is a world without Alzheimer's."

4. **Seafood Restaurant:** "We will be rated a 'five star' restaurant in the Greater Toronto area."

5. **Starbucks:** In 1987 Howard Schultz, CEO of Starbucks, went to Chicago and opened the first Starbucks store in that city. Walking down the street with a colleague, he said that in five years' time everyone will be walking around with a Starbucks cup in their hand.

Each of these vision statements is clear, simple, and easy to see. In high performing teams and organizations, all employees are aligned and focused on the vision or long-term goal.

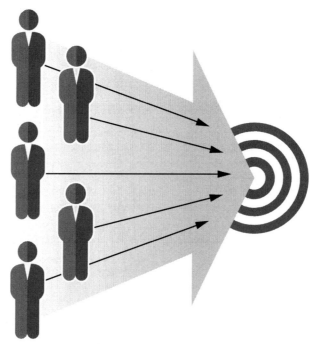

© Kendall Hunt Publishing Company

VALUES

The core values (rules, standards, guidelines) of a company express fundamental beliefs about what's most important regarding people, process (how we will work together), and performance. Values provide the framework needed to set priorities, work together, and make decisions.

Values also describe performance standards such as excellence, continuous improvement, providing great service, etc. Kevin Drumm, PhD, President Broome Community College has a sign on his office wall that lists the following four words: *Learning, Honesty, Integrity, Respect.* Kevin states, "These are the values of the college. On a day to day basis I try to live these values by communicating from the heart, walking the talk, and not shooting the messenger."

Ineffective Values Statement

Some problems with company values include:

   ► **Hollow words:** Enron Corporation proclaimed their company values included—*Respect, Integrity, Compassion, and Excellence.* Senior leaders didn't practice what they preached. They lied to their employees and stockholders.

Some companies post their values in every conference room. That's fine, but "values" need to be practiced, modeled, and lived day-to-day. Employees observe managers and leaders to see if their actions match the company's values.

   ► **Too many values:** Having a laundry list of values or operating principles is not effective. I agree with Jim Collins and Jerry Porras. In their book, *Built to Last: Successful Habits of Visionary Companies,* they make the point that the best companies have only a few core values, usually between one and five. Employees have a hard time trying to remember and live by a set of twelve values. Keep it simple.

Effective Values Statement

Some companies that have a small number of clearly defined set of values include:

1. **Caribou Coffee**

   ▶ Be Excellent

   ▶ Act with Urgency

   ▶ Make a Connection

   ▶ Anticipate Needs

2. **Southwest Airlines**

   ▶ Value 1: Work should be fun . . . it can be play . . . enjoy it

   ▶ Value 2: Work is important . . . don't spoil it with seriousness

   ▶ Value 3: People are important . . . each one makes a difference

3. **Nordstrom**

   ▶ Service to the customer above all else

   ▶ Hard work and individual productivity

   ▶ Never being satisfied

   ▶ Excellence in reputation; being part of something special

4. **Whole Food Markets**

   Three principles define how the store operates:

   ▶ The first principle is all work is teamwork.

   ▶ The second principle is anything worth doing is worth measuring.

   ▶ The third principle is—be your own toughest competitor.

5. **Harley Davidson**

   ▶ Tell the truth

   ▶ Be fair

   ▶ Keep your promises

   ▶ Respect the individual

   ▶ Encourage intellectual curiosity

Managers must not only model the desired behaviors but also hold employees accountable to living the company values.

THE MANAGER'S MISSION, VISION, AND VALUES

Managers need a solid foundation from which to operate. They need to be clear on their personal mission, vision, and values. This foundation will influence how they work with and through people.

► The **mission** of every manager is to efficiently and effectively utilize all resources to meet or exceed customer expectations.

► Each manager needs to articulate a clear and compelling **vision** describing where the team is going and how they will get there.

► Some of the common **values** all managers need include: integrity, fairness, optimism, respect, and continuous improvement.

As a manager you must be crystal clear on who you are and what you stand for. Your mission, vision, and values provide the framework for you to make decisions and achieve goals.

SUMMARY

The one thing you need to remember . . .

A company's and a manager's mission, vision, and values provide the foundation from which they operate. You can't build or create something great without a solid foundation.

DISCUSSION QUESTIONS

1. A community college in New England had the following mission statement: "Education contributes to the quality of life and living, and therefore, the College employs the highest standards in the delivery of its unique and diversified programs and services to its customers. The college assists individuals to develop the capacity for critical thinking; the ability to communicate effectively; an appreciation of the arts, sciences and humanities; and an understanding of the technological nature of modern society."

    a. Assignment: Create a shorter and simpler mission statement for this college. Try to develop a one-sentence, eight- to ten-word mission statement.

2. Assume you are the president of a large company and you classify your manager's performance in these three categories. What action would you take for each group?

    a. Group 1 Managers: hit their numbers and lived by the company's values.

    b. Group 2 Managers: did not hit their numbers but lived the company's values.

    c. Group 3 Managers: hit their numbers but did not live by the company's values.

3. List your top three, most important values. How do you live and practice those values day-to-day?

Chapter 4

BUSINESS STRATEGY

What's our strategy?

What's our competitive advantage?

Strategy refers to the plan or approach a company uses to compete and succeed in the marketplace.

In my neighborhood there are six pizza shops. Each pizza shop needs a strategy as to how it will attract and retain customers. Author and Harvard Professor Michael Porter once said, "Strategy is how to be unique, distinctive, and gain an advantage over the competition." A strategy is judged successful if it leads to a strong competitive position, business growth, and good profit margins.

> "That strategy is a singular thing; there is one strategy for a given business—not a set of strategies. It is one integrated set of choices: what is our winning aspiration; where will we play; how will we win; what capabilities need to be in place; and what management systems must be instituted?"
>
> —Roger L Martin, former Dean of the Rotman School of Management at the University of Toronto

Here are some examples of strategy:

- ▶ **Wal-Mart's** strategy is to sell good quality, name brand, modestly priced merchandise in a clean, no-frills setting that offers one-stop family shopping.
- ▶ **Singapore Airlines** has a strategy based on brand image for the highest quality and luxury customer service. When companies establish value for a brand name it leads to premium pricing.
- ▶ **Enterprise Rent-a-Car** achieved success by pursuing a strategy that its rivals chose to ignore—renting cars to people whose cars are being serviced or are out of commission because of accidents.

> ▶ **Yum Brands**, which includes Taco Bell, KFC, and Pizza Hut recently pursued a strategy of having two of their brands in each store location.
>
> ▶ **Mediterranean** is a new restaurant in my town that offers a low-fat menu to appeal to a more health conscious customer base.

STRATEGIC PLANNING

The senior management team (president and vice-presidents) is responsible for establishing and implementing the company's strategy. Strategic planning involves looking at the target market; trends in the environment; evaluating the company's strengths and weaknesses; and making thoughtful choices about which products and services to offer. It also identifies what a business needs to stop doing.

During strategic planning sessions, the senior team discusses the items listed below. Consultants and facilitators are often hired to help them systematically work through these topics.

1. Target Market

The target market is the group who buys your product or service. The target market may be defined in terms such as gender, age, occupation, economic status, education, geographic location, and so forth. The senior team discusses questions, such as:

▶ What trends are impacting the target market?

▶ Has the target market changed?

▶ What are their unmet needs?

▶ Is our competitive advantage still relevant?

2. Competition

▶ What actions did competitors take in the last six to twelve months?

▶ What will competitors do in the future?

▶ Are there new competitors on the horizon?

3. Major Trends

What are the major economic, political, social, and technological trends that are impacting our customers, employees, suppliers, and competitors?

4. SWOT Analysis

Strategic planning often involves doing a SWOT analysis of both your company and your key competitors. **SWOT** is an acronym that stands for Strengths, Weaknesses, Opportunities, and Threats. The technique is credited to Albert Humphrey, who led a research project at Stanford University in the 1960s and 1970s.

> ▶ **Strengths:** A company's strengths could include things such as its culture, patents, superior technologies, efficient manufacturing technologies, senior management team, and having a unique product distribution system.

▶ **Weaknesses:** Weaknesses could include things such as high turnover, lack of production capacity, and inexperienced managers.

▶ **Opportunities:** What opportunities exist for new products and services? What opportunities exist to be more efficient? Are there opportunities for acquisitions, mergers, or new partnerships that might make sense?

▶ **Threats:** What initiatives is the competition pursuing? Are there threats of new competitors entering the market? Are there substitute products or services that could impact sales?

5. Competitive Advantage

Quite simply, what does the company do better than the competition? Dr. Fred Wiersema, author of *The Discipline of Market Leaders,* recommends that companies should try to do one thing better than anybody in the industry. Make sure the one thing you do better than the competition is something your customers value. It's best to have a competitive advantage that your competitor cannot easily imitate. For example, if you open a basic burger restaurant, a competitor can move in next to you and offer the same products. Your restaurant needs to be unique and not easily copied.

Companies often promote their competitive advantage in their advertisements. For example, Wal-Mart's ads promise customers "everyday low prices."

Here are several examples of the competitive advantage some companies enjoy.

▶ Quality Products: products that have the best performance and reliability. (Honda and Lexus)
▶ Price: offer lower prices than your competition. (Wal-Mart, Price Chopper, and Dollar Store)
▶ Location: provide more convenient locations for customers. (Subway and Dunkin Donuts)
▶ Selection: offer a wider range of choices or unique items. (Whole Foods Market, Trader Joe's, Home Depot, and Lowes)
▶ Service: provide better, more personalized customer service. (Ritz Carlton Hotels and 5-star restaurants)
▶ Speed: provide products or services more quickly than the competition. (Jiffy Lube, McDonald's, Burger King, and other fast-food operations)
▶ Innovation: provide cutting edge products and services. (Apple Computer and 3M)
▶ Safety: products and services that are known for their safety features. (Volvo)

Once senior management defines the company's competitive advantage, they need to focus on the core competencies the employees would need to make it happen. For example, if my competitive advantage is "providing great customer service" most employees will need *Great People Skill.* All of the human resource processes need to support the efforts to recruit, train, and motivate people who will excel at providing great customer service.

Courtesy of Paul B. Thornton

MAKING A PROFIT

Your business strategy needs to produce a profit. Burger King used to have an ad that said, "…*have it your way!*" When I asked if that included getting a free meal, the person taking my order quickly said, "No." Burger King, like every other business, needs to make a profit to stay in operation. There are numerous methods companies use to make a profit. These are often referred to as the "business model" the company is using. Here are some examples:

- ▶ **High volume–low profit margin** (Campbell soups)
- ▶ **Low volume–high profit margin** (Rolex watches, 100-foot yachts, heavy equipment manufacturers)
- ▶ **Subscription:** Customers must pay to join to have access to products and services. (Netflix, Cosco, BJ, the local country club)
- ▶ **Charge businesses to advertise on your website** (Google)
- ▶ **Renting** (apartments, cars, boat slips, equipment, etc.)
- ▶ **Lease out space:** Some gas stations/convenience stores lease out space to a Dunkin Donuts and Subway as a way to add revenue and appeal to more customers

Some companies break even on the initial sale and then make money on the maintenance and upgrades of the equipment.

It's important for every manager to understand their company's strategy and how they make money.

STRATEGIC GOALS AND PLANS

Strategic goals are longer term and are focused on the total organization. One approach used to establish strategic goals is called the balanced scorecard. It was developed by Dr. Robert Kaplan and Dr. David Norton.

The balanced scorecard focuses on the need to establish strategic goals in four areas: financial, business processes, learning and growth, and customer satisfaction. Yes, all companies have financial goals. The balanced scorecard approach provides a clear prescription as to the other goals that influence a company's performance.

- ▶ **Learning and Growth:** Strategic goals in this area relate to employee training and development.
- ▶ **Internal Business Processes:** Strategic goals in this area relate to improving the efficiency of key internal business processes.
- ▶ **Customer Satisfaction:** Strategic goals in this area relate to market share, customer loyalty, and customer satisfaction.
- ▶ **Financial:** Strategic goals in this area relate to revenue, profit, and cash flow.

Look at it this way, learning and growth impacts your internal business processes. As employees gain knowledge and skills, they take steps to improve their processes. Better processes increase customer satisfaction. Happy customers keep buying your products, which keep the financials going in the right direction.

Strategic goals require strategic plans. These are major initiatives that impact the total organization. At the organization level strategic plans include things like acquisitions, reengineering major processes, quality programs, expanding into new markets, and company-wide training programs.

DEPARTMENT INITIATIVES

You'll often hear comments like the following:

- ▶ Our marketing initiative is . . .
- ▶ The selling and distribution strategy is . . .
- ▶ Our new CRM (Customer Relationship Management) initiative is . . .

Each function or department such as sales, production, marketing, human resources, etc., must develop initiatives (plans) that align and support the overall strategic goals. Department initiatives are often referred to as projects, programs, or tactics. There are a limited number of initiatives a department can do well. So it's very important to have clear priorities and a focus on a limited number of initiatives that will produce the desired results.

Once an organization's strategy and department initiatives are established, they must be communicated to all employees. To be understood, they must be clear and simple.

IMPLEMENTATION

Having a strategy and clear initiatives is one thing; implementing them is another story. Implementation refers to all the resources and detailed actions needed to make it happen. Implementation is where the rubber meets the road. Successful implementation requires specific goals and deadlines; clear accountabilities; proper measures and monitoring; incentives and rewards; and, of course, great managers and leaders.

> "Without strategy, execution is useless. Without execution, strategy is useless."
>
> —Morris Chang, CEO of TSMC

Once the organizational strategy and key initiatives are in place, the next big question involves structure. How should people and other resources be organized to implement the strategy and key initiatives? This will be discussed in the next chapter.

SUMMARY

The important things you, the manager need to understand . . .

- ▶ The company's strategy, business model, and competitive advantage.
- ▶ How your department and team initiatives support the overall company strategy.

DISCUSSION QUESTIONS

1. Do a Google search on the Boston Consulting Group's four product types—Stars, Cash Cows, Dogs, and Question Marks. Define what is meant by each product type.

2. What is your personal competitive advantage? What are the one or two traits/abilities that separate you from the crowd?

3. **HENRY'S HEALTH FOODS CHAIN CASE STUDY**

> You have been working as the human resources manager for Henry's Health Foods. It is a medium-sized chain of health food stores on the West Coast. There are about thirty stores spread over five states. Henry's Health Foods sells a variety of products, including vitamins, organic fruits and vegetables, canned goods, nuts, and dried fruit.
>
> On Monday morning, your boss, Gloria Dunn, invites you into her office and informs you that Henry's Health Foods is going to close its doors and become a virtual store. All customers will make purchases over the Internet. Dunn tells you, "This is obviously a major change in strategy. There are significant people issues, but I don't want you to worry. You will remain my HR manager in the new organization. I'd like you to help me understand all of the people implications of this new strategy."
>
> After you leave her office, you begin to think about some of the implications of what your boss said. In terms of people, there would no longer be a need for certain jobs. At the same time, this change would vastly increase the need for some new jobs. For example, warehousing and shipping will need to be included in the new organization.
>
> Henry's Health Foods currently employs sixty part-time stockers, thirty full-time cashiers, fifteen full-time store managers, fifteen part-time assistant store managers, two accountants, one financial analyst, one marketing manager, two information systems staff members, and three purchasing employees.

   a. How can the company use the new strategy to establish a competitive advantage?

   b. What employee competencies are required to achieve this competitive advantage?

4. **FAIRVIEW INN CASE STUDY**

> Fairview Inn, a national hotel chain with over 7,000 employees, implemented a *100% Satisfaction Guarantee* policy to help it gain a competitive advantage in a highly competitive industry. The guarantee is simple; if guests are not completely satisfied with every aspect of their stay, they are not expected to pay. Bottom line, Fairview Inn's employees are supposed to do whatever it takes to satisfy guests—including giving them their money back.
>
> A Fairview Inn housekeeper said, "My job includes cleaning and preparing guestrooms but the bigger job is to satisfy guests. For example, if I see a guest having a problem with the lock on her room door, I have the authority to stop what I'm doing and take whatever action is necessary to correct the situation." Another housekeeper added, "Yesterday I spent an hour helping a customer who was having a problem. Naturally, my regular work was behind schedule. My supervisor chewed me out for not getting a room ready on time."
>
> The inn manager states, "I believe in our 100% satisfaction guarantee. That's what I expect as a customer. However, I don't want employees giving away the store."

a. Is a *100% Satisfaction Guarantee* an effective strategy/competitive advantage for the Fairview Inn?

b. What core competencies are needed in order to implement this strategy?

Chapter 5

ORGANIZATIONAL STRUCTURE

What is the difference between the formal and informal structure?

Is there one best organizational structure that all companies should be using?

Once the organizational strategy is in place, the next big question involves structure. How should people and other resources be organized? The corporate structure is created in order to implement a given company strategy. The phrase "structure follows strategy" was first proposed by the historian Alfred Chandler.

There are many ways to organize employees and resources including by function, by teams, by product line, by geographic region, by customers, etc. There is no one best way to organize your resources.

ORGANIZATIONAL CHARTS

Business leaders use organizational charts to illustrate the formal structure of the organization. These charts use boxes to represent the various departments and positions in the organization. Usually only management levels are shown. Lines connecting the boxes indicate who reports to whom.

The organizational chart has two dimensions: one representing vertical hierarchy and one representing horizontal specialization.

- ► **Vertical hierarchy** establishes the chain of command, or who reports to whom. Chain of command refers to the flow of authority from one level of the organization to the next. The formal communications channel follows the chain of command.
- ► **Horizontal specialization** establishes the division of labor. The various departments and work groups identify how the work is divided.

Some of the other terms used to describe the structure of organizations include:

- ► **Line vs. Staff:** Line departments perform tasks that reflect the organization's primary mission. In a manufacturing organization, the line departments are involved in designing, developing, producing, marketing, and selling the products. Line departments typically include engineering, operations, sales, and marketing. Staff departments are those that help and support the line departments. Staff departments include strategic planning, research and development, accounting, finance, and human resources.

▶ **The Unity of Command principle** maintains that each employee should have only one supervisor. When employees receive orders from several bosses, it creates confusion and difficulty prioritizing tasks.

▶ **Span of Control** refers to the number of direct reports a manager has. Having less than four direct reports is considered a narrow span of control. Having more than twelve direct reports is considered a broad span of control. The number of direct reports is influenced by factors such as:

— *Similarity of functions:* The more similar the tasks performed by employees, the possibility of a larger span of control.

— *Complexity:* The simpler the tasks performed by subordinates, the greater the span of control can be.

— *Change:* Frequent or rapid changes in jobs tasks and quality requirements may require a small span of control.

— *Coordination:* When there is a great deal of coordination required between and among employees, a smaller span of control may be appropriate.

▶ **Tall vs. Flat Structure:** This refers to the number of levels of management in an organization. A tall structure has narrow spans of control and many levels of management. A flat structure has wide spans of control and fewer levels of management. Today's trend is toward flatter organizational structures. There are fewer managers and each is responsible for a large number of employees.

▶ **Centralization vs. Decentralization:** This pertains to the management level at which decisions are made. In centralized organizations, decision-making is done at the top level. The president and vice presidents make most if not all of the decisions. Decentralization means decision-making authority is pushed downward to lower organizational levels. In a highly decentralized organization, first-line managers have the power to make many decisions.

> Sam Walton, the late founder of Wal-Mart once said, "The bigger we get as a company, the more important it becomes to shift responsibility and authority toward the front lines, toward that department manager who's stocking the shelves and talking to the customer."

▶ **Formal vs. Informal** refers to the degree to which there are rules and regulations all employees must follow. In a formal organization, there are explicit job descriptions, lots of rules, and adherence to the chain of command. In an informal organization, there are fewer rules and policies and a more casual environment.

FUNCTIONAL STRUCTURE

The functional organizational structure is the most common way companies organize work and workers. The chart on the following page illustrates a typical functional structure. In this structure, the president has P&L (profit and loss) responsibilities. Each function or department is headed by a vice president. Below the vice president are one or more managers who manage the employees who are doing the work of that department.

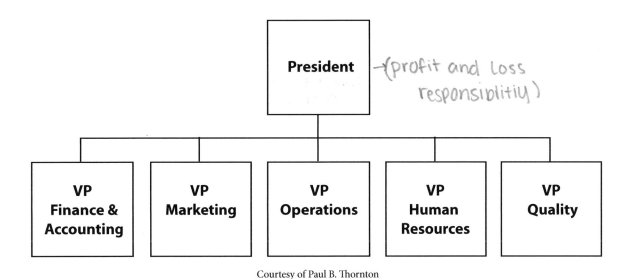

Courtesy of Paul B. Thornton

In addition to the departments listed on the above organizational chart, other departments you may find in large companies include customer service, engineering, information systems, sales, legal, and community relations.

Of course, not all companies have the same functions. An insurance company and an advertising agency both have sales, accounting, human resources, and information systems departments. But an advertising agency may also have creative, print, electronic, and web-related advertising departments. An insurance company may have separate departments for life, auto, home, and health insurance. The kind of functional departments a company has depends, in part, on the business or industry it is in.

Advantages of a Functional Structure

1. Allows work to be done by highly qualified specialists.

2. Provides a job ladder that people can advance through.

3. Lowers costs by reducing duplication.

4. Increases efficiency and effectiveness of communication and coordination within the department.

Disadvantages of a Functional Structure

1. Cross-department coordination can be difficult.

2. Managers and employees are often more interested in doing what's right for their function than in doing what's right for the customer or the organization as a whole.

3. Functional departments often produce managers and workers with narrow experience and expertise. Some employees stay in one function for the bulk of their career.

MATRIX STRUCTURE

The matrix organizational structure is used in a variety of settings including manufacturing companies and businesses that have multiple product lines.

In a matrix structure, most employees belong to at least two formal groups at the same time—a functional group and a product or project team. They also have two bosses—one within the function and the other within the team.

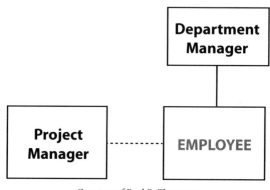

Courtesy of Paul B. Thornton

For example, say a clothing manufacturer uses a matrix structure. They produce several products: product A is footwear, product B is outerwear, product C is sleepwear, and so on. Each product line serves a different market and customers. The company must effectively use people from manufacturing, design, and marketing to work on each product line. Each product manager has profit and loss responsibilities for his product line.

When a new customer order is received for outerwear, several employees from design, finance, and production are assigned to that project. They become the group responsible for the design, development, and delivery of the order. When the order is completed, the employees return to their functional departments and wait to be assigned to a new project. In most matrix organizations employees are assigned to multiple projects at the same time. Employees are constantly juggling their time and attention on a number of projects.

Advantages of Matrix Structures

1. Better cooperation across functions.

2. Improved decision-making as problem-solving takes place at the team level, where the best information is available.

3. Better customer service, since there is always a product or project manager informed and available to answer questions.

Disadvantages of Matrix Structures

1. The two-boss system is susceptible to power struggles, as functional supervisors and project managers vie with one another to exercise authority.

2. The two-boss system can be frustrating if it creates task confusion and conflicting work priorities.

3. There are issues with performance appraisals. Who does them—the functional manager or the project manager? In most organizations the functional boss is assigned that responsibility. The functional manager is required to get feedback from each project manager that the employee has worked for during the evaluation period. But that doesn't always happen. Some employees complain that their functional boss doesn't fully understand the contributions they're making. This can lead to unhappy employees and morale issues.

TEAM STRUCTURES

Organizations with team structures use both permanent and temporary teams to solve problems, complete special projects, and accomplish day-to-day tasks. Many companies use cross-functional teams to deal with company-wide problems and to create a plan to pursue new opportunities.

Here are some examples of companies that use teams as a way to organize their employees.

► Each of the Whole Foods Market stores has ten self-managed teams: produce, grocery, prepared foods, etc. Each team has a designated leader and performance goals. The team leaders in each store are a team; store leaders in each region are a team; and the company's regional presidents are a team.

► At SEI INVESTMENTS, the entire organization is operated by 140 self-directed teams.

► At Nucor Steel, production workers are organized into teams ranging in size from eight to forty employees.

► Oticon Holding A/S is a Danish hearing aid manufacturer. At Oticon, a hundred or so projects exist at any one time. Most employees work on several project teams at once. This is an open market system where project leaders compete for resources, and employees compete for a place on desirable projects. Each employee has a computer and a desk on wheels. This allows any employee to move his or her "office" anywhere else in the building in just five minutes.

Advantages of Team Structures

1. They break down the functional silos and create more effective lateral relations for problem-solving, learning from others, collaborating, and getting the work done.

2. Most employees report experiencing a greater sense of involvement and enjoy the interaction with other employees.

3. More learning can occur. As team members share their insights and knowledge, all team members grow and develop.

Disadvantages of Team Structures

1. It can take a long time for a group to become an effective team. Team members must learn to trust each other, deal with conflicts, collaborate, and establish common goals.

2. Teams can spend a lot of time in meetings that aren't always productive.

NETWORK STRUCTURES

Organizations using a network structure operate around a central core. This core is linked through "networks" of relationships with outside companies that supply essential services. In this structure, organizations retain only the most essential or "core" components that give them a competitive advantage and outsource the rest.

In some networked organizations, the firm—itself—is very small, consisting of a relatively small number of full-time core employees working from a central headquarters. Beyond that, it is structured as a network of partner relationships, maintained operationally by using the latest information technology. Some of the most commonly outsourced functions include advertising, accounting, human resources, payroll, and manufacturing.

> When Galoob Toys, Inc. selects a toy for its product line, it contracts with a firm to manufacture and package the product. The toys are then shipped to the United States. They are distributed by commissioned manufacturers' representatives. Even accounts receivable are handled by an outside credit firm. The president and executive vice president spend their time making critical decisions and coordinating with the various organizations on which they depend. You might say Galoob is an *"idea and coordination business."* The business makes money by selling toys even though the toys are never touched by an employee of Galoob.

Advantages of a Network Structure

1. They are lean and streamlined. They help organizations stay cost-competitive through reduced overhead and increased operating efficiency.

2. You can utilize other companies that have expertise in areas in which you don't excel.

Disadvantages of a Network Structure

1. Relationships with the outsourced companies can be challenging and problematic. It may be difficult to maintain quality standards and receive timely delivery of products and information.

2. If one part of the network breaks down or fails to deliver, the entire system may suffer.

3. A lack of loyalty can develop when contractors are used infrequently.

INVERTED PYRAMID STRUCTURE

The inverted pyramid structure turns the traditional organizational chart upside down. Also, you'll note the customer is at the top of the chart. It is a powerful reminder to all employees—never forget the importance of the customer.

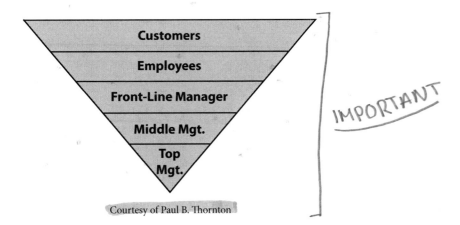

Courtesy of Paul B. Thornton

IMPORTANT

It also implies that the most important people in the organization are the people who deal with the customers. Managers need to understand a key part of their job is training, developing, helping, and taking care of the people who take care of the customers. In other words, managers work for the people who report to them. Managers need to be asking the people above them on the chart, "What can I do to help you perform at your best?" In this structure managers spend less time telling people what to do and more time serving people. Instead of treating your employees as a resource who works for you, you shift to being a resource for them.

Some of the companies that operate using the inverted pyramid structure include Nordstrom, Chic-fil-A, Southwest Airlines, and WD-40. In these organizations, front line employees are empowered to do what they think is required to satisfy the customer.

To summarize, companies use a variety of formal structures to organize their resources including: functional, matrix, teams, networks, and the invented pyramid. The formal structure can provide useful information about levels of management, spans of control, formal communication channels, and how work gets done.

THE INFORMAL (SOCIAL) NETWORK

But organizations are much more than just the formal structure. They also have an informal social network. Harold S. Geneen once said, "Every company has two organizational structures: the formal one is written on the charts; the other is the everyday relationship of the men and women in the organization."

The chart on the following page is an example of an informal network. The lines represent the day-to-day interactions and communication patterns between and among people. Some connections may be purely social, while others may be seeking advice or guidance for work-related issues. The connections in the network can be strongly or weakly linked.

→ the day to day interactions and communications between and among people.

The informal network or structure that develops is based on social relationships, friendships, alliances, common interests, and common enemies.

Information can be transmitted through the informal network (or grapevine) in any direction: up, down, diagonally, or horizontally across the organizational structure. The grapevine is completely separate from the company's formal communication channels and is sometimes much faster spreading a message.

SUMMARY

Several things you need to remember . . .

- ▶ There is no one best way to organize people and resources.
- ▶ Each organizational structure has advantages and disadvantages.
- ▶ Both the formal structure and informal networks provide useful information for managers.

DISCUSSION QUESTIONS

1. What are the issues that result from too big of a span of control and from too small of a span of control?

2. At a state university, what things should be centralized and what things should be decentralized?

3. **PAUL'S PIZZA CASE STUDY**

> Paul's Pizza Corporation operates pizza stores in several northeast cities. Company headquarters is located in Boston, Massachusetts. Each pizza store manager reports to the VP-Operations at the corporate office. The company's mission statement is the following: *Provide the best tasting pizza at the best price at the best location.*
>
> Each pizza store has one manager, a day assistant manager, and two night assistant managers. There are no systematic criteria for being a manager. Managers are selected from the ranks of assistant managers. Assistant managers are chosen for their ability to perform the duties of the regular employees.
>
> The employees are mostly college students, with a few high school students performing the less challenging jobs. All the employees, with the exception of the managers, are part-time. During the day, there are seven part-time workers. At night there are eight part-time workers reporting to each assistant night manager.

a. Draw an organizational chart for one of the pizza stores in this corporation.

b. What is the span of control for the assistant manager who works days?

c. How many levels of management are there in this corporation?

Part III

THE MANAGER

What do managers believe about themselves and the people they manage?

What type of management style works best?

Should managers just tell employees what to do?

Why is delegation so challenging?

What type of power do managers have?

Is it possible to develop charisma or personal power?

What are some of the tactics managers can use to influence others?

What are the different approaches leaders use to influence and inspire change?

Chapters 6 through 9 will help answer these questions.

Managers work with and through others to achieve various goals. Each manager needs to use his or her power, influence, and management style to help people perform at their best.

© alphaspirit/Shutterstock.com

Chapter 6

CORE BELIEFS AND BEHAVIOR

What are some of the core beliefs and behavior of all effective managers?

This I believe…

Managers have a set of core beliefs about people, teams, leading others, and what it takes to be successful. You can't manage or lead if you don't know what you believe in and stand for. Every manager must spend time in reflection and self-examination to identify what they truly believe and value. Their beliefs get tested and fine-tuned over time.

A person's core beliefs will influence the approach he or she uses to manage and lead. Here are some quotes that describe one or more core beliefs of some successful managers and leaders.

- ► "Employees are a company's greatest asset—they're your competitive advantage. You want to attract and retain the best; provide them with encouragement, stimulus, and make them feel that they are an integral part of the company's mission."—Anne M. Mulcahy
- ► "Research indicates that workers have three prime needs: Interesting work, recognition for doing a good job, and being let in on things that are going on in the company."—Zig Ziglar
- ► "Where performance is measured, performance improves. Where performance is measured and reported, the rate of improvement accelerates."—Thomas S. Monson
- ► "A corporation is a living organism; it has to continue to shed its skin. Methods have to change. Focus has to change. Values have to change. The sum total of those changes is transformation."—Andy Grove
- ► "There is only one boss. The customer. And he can fire everybody in the company from the chairman on down, simply by spending his money somewhere else."—Sam Walton
- ► "An organization's ability to learn, and translate that learning into action rapidly, is the ultimate competitive advantage."—Jack Welch
- ► "You must be the change you want to see in the world."—Mahatma Gandhi
- ► "In matters of style, swim with the current; in matters of principle, stand like a rock."—President Thomas Jefferson

► "Make your product easier to buy than your competition, or you will find your customers buying from them, not you."—Mark Cuban

► "Great leaders are almost always great simplifiers, who can cut through argument, debate, and doubt to offer a solution everybody can understand."—General Colin Powell

► "The first responsibility of a leader is to define reality. The last is to say thank you. In between, the leader is a servant."—Max De Pree

► "Leadership is lifting a person's vision to higher sights, the raising of a person's performance to a higher standard, the building of a personality beyond its normal limitations."—Peter F. Drucker

OFFICE WALL QUOTES

Some leaders post one or more of their core beliefs on their office wall or keep them on their desk. For example, W. Clement Stone began as a shoeshine boy and became a multimillionaire. He credits his success to three words: **Do It Now.** He required everyone who worked for him to write those words on index cards and post them in their work area.

© wow.subtropica/Shutterstock.com

Here are some additional examples of what people had or have in their office as reminders of what's important.

► **"It can be done!"**—Sign President Ronald Reagan kept on his desk in the Oval Office.

► **"Attitude is everything!"** —Sign in red letters on the desk of Carol Leary, PhD, President, Bay Path College.

► **"Successful People are the Few Who Focus in and Follow Through"**—Sign in the office of Stew Leonard, Jr., President, Stew Leonard's Dairy. Leaders don't just talk about change; they implement change.

► **"Start Talking and Get to Work"**—Sign in the office of Alden Davis, former Business Effectiveness Consultant, Pratt & Whitney Division of United Technologies Corporation.

- ► **"Be Realistic, Demand the Impossible"**—Sign in the office of T. J. Rodgers, founder and CEO of Cypress Semiconductor.

- ► **"A desk is a dangerous place from which to view the world." John le Carré**—Sign in the office of Louis V. Gerstner, Jr., former CEO of IBM.

- ► **"I'm Responsible"**—Sign on the desk of Rudy Giuliani, who was the mayor of New York City from 1994–2001.

- ► **"The time is always right to do what is right." Martin Luther King Jr.** —Sign on the office wall of Michael Jansma, President GEMaffair.com.

- ► **"Leaders should be able to Stand Alone, Take the Heat, Bear the Pain, Tell the Truth, and Do What's Right." Max De Pree**—Sign in the office of Brian Morehouse, coach of women's basketball at Hope College, 2006 Division III National Champions.

THEORY X & Y

Managers also make assumptions about people, business trends, and what customers will want in the future. One well-known set of assumptions about employees was developed by Douglas McGregor, a social psychologist. In his book, *The Human Side of Enterprise*, he proposed a set of assumptions about people which he labeled Theory X and Theory Y.

- ► **Theory X** assumes the average worker:
  - — dislikes work and attempts to avoid it
  - — prefers to be directed
  - — avoids responsibility
  - — wants security above all else

Theory X managers see employees as inferior, immature, unmotivated, and not to be trusted. When managers hold Theory X assumptions, they assign tasks on a piecemeal basis and micromanage. In addition, they frequently criticize their employees' work and tell them they are lazy and irresponsible.

- ► **Theory Y** assumes the average worker:
  - — finds work fulfilling and enjoyable
  - — is self-directed to meet objectives if he/she is committed to them
  - — seeks and accepts responsibility
  - — wants to learn, grow, and develop

Theory Y managers treat every employee as if he or she has great talent and potential. When managers hold Theory Y assumptions, they provide employees with challenging assignments, freedom to do their jobs, and frequent coaching. Also, they praise their accomplishments and build their confidence every chance they get.

SELF-FULFILLING PROPHESY

The self-fulfilling prophecy maintains that "what you expect is what you get." High expectations lead to high performance; low expectations lead to low performance.

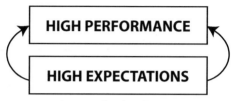

Courtesy of Paul B. Thornton

People tend to respond positively to a manager's high expectations and confidence in their abilities. If you expect people to be "winners" and you actually treat them like "winners," pretty soon they start to act like "winners." As people achieve assigned goals they are given more responsibilities which leads to growth and development. The opposite is also true. If a leader's expectations are low, employee productivity is likely to be poor. More often than not people do what they think they are expected to do.

> My math teacher believed his students had great talent and potential. He set high standards and was very demanding. My English teacher was the opposite. He expected very little from his students. For the most part, my performance matched my teacher's expectations.

FIRM BUT OPEN

Successful managers have firm beliefs about business, managing people and what it takes to achieve success. Their beliefs drive their day-to-day behavior. But they are also open to new ideas and trying new things. In some cases when they try new behaviors it influences their beliefs.

There is an old debate about which is true, that—"beliefs drive behavior" or "behavior drives beliefs." As you have learned in this chapter, both are correct.

SUMMARY

Things you need to remember . . .

- ► Know who you are and what you believe.
- ► Be open to new ideas and experiences.

DISCUSSION QUESTIONS

1. What would you post on your office wall?

2. What is the fine line between setting expectations too high and too low?

Chapter 7

MANAGEMENT STYLES

How many different management styles are there?

Is there one best management style which every manager should use?

Management styles are useful when thinking about alternative ways managers interact with people to get things done.

I believe there are three basic styles of managing—directing, discussing, and delegating. The most effective managers use a style that is appropriate for the situation, which is based upon people's knowledge and skills, the nature of the required change, time constraints, and other factors. They know what to do when using each style.

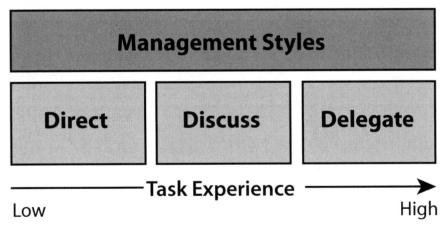

Courtesy of Paul B. Thornton

Some points to consider before deciding which style to use.

► How much experience does the employee have in performing a particular task?

► Is the employee able to do the task? Do they have the necessary knowledge and skills?

► Is the person motivated to do the task?

The goal is to use a management style that fits the needs of the employee relative to the task he or she is assigned. Using an appropriate management style helps employees learn, grow, and become more independent.

My boss always seemed to know what I needed. When I needed structure, he provided detailed directions. On other projects he delegated. He gave me the freedom to figure it out on my own.

—Peter, Human Resources Trainee

THE DIRECTING STYLE

The manager establishes goals, assigns responsibilities, sets standards, and defines expectations. The directing style is appropriate when employees lack experience and don't know what to do. It's also appropriate when there is a mandate from senior management that describes *what* must be done and *how* it must be done. The manager is the "commander-in-charge," simply carrying out these orders. The directing style is also appropriate in emergency situations. Good direction also includes specifics around non-negotiable items such as safety and ethics.

"Like throwing a rock in a pond, I try to stretch people one ripple at a time. When challenges are given, I provide people with a backdrop to put the goal in context. People want to know why their company cares about this specific goal and why they should care. I also find it helpful to describe what it will be like a year from now if the goal is accomplished."

—Sue Lewis, former Vice President and Chief Real Estate Officer, The Travelers

---

Start with the big picture. Provide the context before launching into specifics. State clearly *what* you expect, *how* you expect it to be done, and *when* it is due. Wordy and poorly organized directions confuse, overwhelm, and frustrate employees. It's important to provide the right amount of detail. Communication breakdowns occur when important details are omitted.

► **Communication** in the directing style is predominantly one-way, from manager to employee. The manager imparts information to the employee via verbal or written instructions. The only feedback the manager looks for is the answer to the question "Do you understand the instructions?" There are times when managers need to be very direct and candid to get through to their employees.

▶ **Coaching** occurs as the manager tells the employees what they need to do or change. In addition, the manager may demonstrate desired behaviors to the employee, such as rewriting an e-mail to improve clarity or showing how to run an effective meeting.

▶ **Decision-making** occurs when the manager defines the problem, evaluates options, and makes a decision. Employees learn how to frame problems, evaluate alternatives, and make effective decisions by understanding the process the manager follows.

▶ **Recognition** happens when the manager praises employees who follow directions and complete assignments as directed. It can be accomplished on a more formal basis through company reward/recognition programs and praise provided in private manager-employee conferences.

Being clear and direct is a good thing. The employee knows what's expected and what he needs to get done. It's also important for managers to hold their employees accountable for completing the assigned tasks. Some of the additional points to remember when using the directing style include:

1. When you need to be direct—be direct. Don't sugarcoat the message.

2. Operate from an "adult-to-adult" framework. Always treat people with respect.

3. Provide written instructions if the directions are complex or lengthy.

4. Test the transfer. Ask the employee to explain his understanding of the directions.

THE DISCUSSING STYLE

The manager encourages critical thinking and lively discussion by asking employees questions about the problem, opportunity, or issue that must be resolved. The manager is a facilitator, guiding the discussion to a logical conclusion. The discussing style is effective when employees have ideas and are willing to speak up. After a productive discussion, specific goals need to be established. The goals may be reached through consensus—both manager and employee agree on the goal or goals may be established by the manager after the discussion. If employees are involved in establishing the goals they are generally more committed to achieving them.

> VP–Operations states,
>
> "I prefer to use a directing style to state the goal so it is clear. When developing the plan I ask questions about the steps the individual thinks are necessary to achieve the goal. This approach creates individual ownership for the plan and the goal. Additionally, creating a plan for implementation provides a roadmap that can be reviewed frequently to make sure that the person is staying on course."

Start by asking general questions. Asking employees for their ideas and opinions increases their engagement in the learning process. "What would you do in this situation?" is more effective at promoting discussion than a question that aims for a single "right" answer. Start with general questions, and then get more specific.

It is best to prepare questions in advance. Great discussions don't just happen.

▶ **Communication** in the discussing style is two-way (between manager and employee) or multi-way (among employees, or among employees and manager). The manager asks challenging questions and listens carefully to the employees' comments. Follow-up questions help uncover underlying assumptions, reasoning, and feelings. Employees learn to have opinions and be able to back them up with facts and data.

▶ **Coaching** occurs when the manager asks questions that require employees to evaluate their own performance. Coaching questions like these are effective: "How do you think you did? What could you have done better? What steps can you take to improve?" The goal is to encourage employees to examine what they did, why they did it, and what they can do to improve.

▶ **Decision-making** occurs as the manager and employees collaborate and work together to define problems, identify and evaluate alternative solutions, and make sound decisions. Employees learn as they respond to the manager's questions, offer their own ideas, and consider the advantages and disadvantages of each option.

▶ **Recognition** may be given to employees who express their ideas clearly and succinctly. In addition, employees should be praised for thoughtful observations, creative ideas, building on the ideas of others, and helping the group reach a logical conclusion.

The discussing style is appropriate when there is adequate time for meetings and participation. Effective managers know that asking the right question at the right time engages people and increases their commitment. Some of the additional points to remember when using the discussing style include:

1. Ask one question at a time.

2. Don't allow one or two employees to dominate the discussion. Solicit everyone's ideas and opinions.

3. After a good discussion, it's important to get closure on who is going to do what tasks by when.

THE DELEGATING STYLE

The manager empowers the employee. The delegating style is appropriate when people have the experience, skills, and motivation to get the job done. Experienced employees don't need a manager telling them how to do it. They want freedom to take action and solve problems on their own.

When using the delegating style, managers direct or discuss *what* needs to be accomplished and by *when* it must be completed. However, the *how-to-do-it* part of the equation is left up to the employee. It is expected that the employee will take action and make decisions as to how the task will be accomplished. Responsibility and authority are given to the employee to make it happen.

Managers should assign tasks that are challenging, but not overwhelming. When employees are empowered, most are inspired and motivated to show what they can do, but some become anxious. Increase the probability of success for each employee by expressing confidence in his or her ability to get the job done.

▶ **Communication** occurs as the manager assigns tasks for employees to tackle independently or in small groups. Employees listen and ask follow-up questions until they fully understand what they need to deliver. Establish check-in dates. Managers need to get periodic updates from employees to insure appropriate progress is being made.

► **Coaching** is accomplished primarily through self-coaching. Employees gain the most maturity and confidence when they are able to critique their own performance. For example, to my employee I might say something like the following: "I want you to think about your performance on this assignment. Identify three things you did well and one area needing improvement. I'd like to meet tomorrow at 10:00 a.m. to hear what you come up with."

► **Decision-making** happens as employees establish goals, implement plans, and work through issues on their own. They learn by doing.

► **Recognition** most often takes the form of praise and other rewards given to employees who work well independently, meet deadlines, and produce quality work.

Bob Emery, Head Hockey Coach, Plattsburg State University stated,

"I coach hockey, but I'm really teaching leadership, life skills, and teamwork. In the old days I used a lot of directing when coaching. 'Do this. Don't do that.' Today I do a lot more discussing and delegating. I ask a lot of questions to see what the player is thinking. I delegate when I want the players to do self-reflection and self-analysis. For example, players must critique their play after each game by watching videotapes. Each player discusses his self-analysis with one of the coaches to make sure we are all on the same page. Coaching is productive when real learning occurs. This happens best when the player is engaged and takes ownership for his performance both on and off the ice."

As employees grow and develop, they want the freedom to make their own decisions and solve their own problems. Such independence promotes maturity and increases motivation. Some of the additional points to remember when using the delegating style include:

1. Don't over-delegate to the same one or two "star" performers.

2. Avoid "reverse delegation." Don't allow employees to give work back to you. The consistent act of reverse delegation trains the employee to know the manager will always finish the job.

3. Never delegate the responsibility for administering discipline or dealing with an employee's personal issues.

4. Make sure a deadline is clearly stated.

At the end of each week, managers should assess their own performance with questions like the following:

► Did I use the most appropriate management style for each situation?

► Am I asking the right questions?

► What else can I delegate?

► Who's ready to take on a bigger task?

► Are employees becoming more capable and independent?

SUMMARY

Some things you need to remember . . .

- ▶ There is no one best style.
- ▶ Use a management style that fits the needs of the situation.
- ▶ Change your style as employees gain experience and develop their skills.

DISCUSSION QUESTIONS

1. A college basketball coach calls a timeout. Explain what the coach would say using each style of management.

2. What is the fine line between being "too direct" and "not direct enough"?

3. What is the difference between "asking questions" and "interrogating the employee"? What is the difference between a genuine question and a rhetorical question?

4. Your hard-working and generally efficient administrative assistant, Sue, has recently been bringing in resumes and cover letters to type for her unemployed husband. He has been out of work for six weeks. This has caused her regular work to be a bit backlogged. Using the directing style of management, what would you say to Sue?

5. You delegated a project to a coworker. You notice he is cutting corners to finish the task more quickly. Although your coworker is cutting corners, his actions may not affect the overall project. What, if anything, would you do?

6. Your highly experienced and capable team is confronted with an emergency. Due to a serious quality problem, all products are being returned to your department. Your team has to re-inspect and return them to various customers within forty-eight hours. What management style would you use? Why? Explain your choice.

7. You have stepped into an efficiently run situation. The previous manager ran a tight ship. He used a directing style of management. All team members have over ten years of experience and are highly trained and capable. What management style would you use? Why? Explain your choice.

8. You have been promoted to the position of marketing manager. The previous manager used a delegating style of management. Team members have adequately handled their tasks and assignments. The team has a good record of accomplishments. However, new, tougher performance standards are required. What do you think your team members will want to know?

9. Joe, the manager, delegated a task to one of his employees. Several days later the employee returns and says, "I don't know how to do it." Joe states, "OK, I'll do it; let me find something else for you to do." What should Joe have done?

10. You have delegated an important project to Jason, one of your direct reports. Fast-forward—the project is over budget and the completion date is six weeks behind schedule. Your boss calls you in and says, "What the hell happened?!" How do you respond?

Chapter 8

POWER AND INFLUENCE

What can managers do to increase their power and influence?

Parents, teachers, coaches, and managers have power. Coaches decide who plays and who sits on the bench. Teachers give assignments and grade performance. Managers determine who gets raises and promotions. In addition, managers have the power to allocate resources, schedule meetings, and require employees to listen to their ideas.

There are three basic types of power:

1. Position

2. Expertise

3. Personal

> "When used correctly, power has the ability to move people to action. As my management responsibilities grew, I acquired more sources of power and constantly focused on improving my leadership skills. As my sources of power increased, my ability to shape the agenda and secure the resources to implement it increased. At the pinnacle of my career, power alone was not enough. The combination of multiple sources of power and effective leadership skills was the difference-maker."
>
> — Mary Jean Thornton, former Executive Vice President & CIO,
> The Travelers Life and Annuity Company

POSITION POWER

Managers gain power as a result of their formal position in the organization. The chain of command gives managers power over the people below. In addition, a manager's position in the hierarchy can give him or her access to resources such as equipment, information, money, and people.

But how much power does a manager have? Paul Hersey and Ken Blanchard, authors of *Management of Organizational Behavior*, make the point that the amount of power you're given depends on the level of trust and confidence your boss has in you. Some bosses want to approve everything, giving the manager very little power to act on their own. But some managers have the attitude—"I'll take action now and ask for forgiveness later."

Managers can use their position power to direct and motivate people by providing rewards, punishments, and sharing information. The actions they can take include:

► **Reward and Recognize**—They can dole out desirable things to employees such as pay increases, bonuses, promotions, public recognition, time off, and opportunities to attend top-tier training programs. Effective use of recognition and rewards can motivate people to put in extra effort. Reward power is effective so long as people value the rewards and see a clear link between their performance and the desired reward.

► **Punish**—They can punish and reprimand people who don't complete assignments, meet expectations, or make required changes. Managers can administer discipline, withhold pay raises, reduce salaries, assign unpleasant tasks, etc.

   Although punishment may lead to temporary compliance, this type of corrective action can produce undesirable side effects such as withdrawal, fear, and unwillingness to take risks.

► **Access**—A manager's position in the organization gives him or her access to information and people. Information is power! Managers can decide how much information to share and with whom. In addition, they can use their network to make introductions, open doors, and connect with people as needed.

   Keep in mind, you need to be fair and consistent when using your position power. The worst managers play favorites. Don't have two sets of standards when it comes to who gets rewarded and who gets punished.

Edward, VP Operations, Insurance Company states,

"My boss, who was president of the company, used his position power to create a loyal inner circle. If you were part of the inner circle you received the big bonuses and pay raises. However, members of this inner circle were a bunch of 'yes people.' These people lost credibility with their staffs and employees in their organizations. Needless to say, the president was very ineffective at developing people to assume key executive and leadership roles."

Some managers simply don't use their power. They never reward or punish any of their employees. Or they only use rewards but not punishments. Some managers do the reverse. They overly rely on punishments and never praise employees. The best managers effectively administer both rewards and punishments.

Position Power and Management Style

What's the relationship between management style and position power? Each style of management involves different degrees of power sharing.

- ▶ *Directing Style*—When managers use the directing style, they retain all the power and control. The manager makes most, if not all, decisions.
- ▶ *Discussing Style*—When managers use the discussing style, they share power with their employees. They engage people and give them power to contribute their ideas in setting goals and solving problems.
- ▶ *Delegating Style*—When managers use the delegation style, they empower people to make their own decisions and take action as needed.

EXPERTISE POWER

What's your expertise?

We listen to the car mechanic, our doctor, and our accountant because they have expertise and credibility. We do what they tell us because we trust and value their advice. These individuals are referred to as SMEs—Subject Matter Experts. They are the go-to people when help and guidance is needed. SMEs can influence people at all levels of the org chart.

Experts are able to simplify the complex; they can explain what's happening and why it's happening in a clear and understandable way. Experts can talk at both the macro level and the detail level.

Some managers have expertise in areas such as recruiting and hiring, running meetings, project management tools, motivating employees, team-building, and the specific likes and dislikes of certain customers. They use their expertise to help others, shape the agenda, and influence important decisions.

Become an expert at one or more things. Use your expertise to promote yourself and become the go-to-person. Some of the ways experts market their expertise is by speaking at conferences; writing books and articles; and offering seminars. To maintain SME status, managers must stay current. It's critical to keep your knowledge and skills up-to-date.

PERSONAL POWER

Managers and leaders with personal power are often described as having *charisma*. When they enter the room, you notice. They make a positive first impression. They project a professional image through dress, grooming, posture, mannerisms, and their communication skills.

People with charisma possess three important, distinguishing characteristics:

1. **Presence**—They are present, or in the moment. They give people their full, undivided attention. *She made me feel like I was the only person in the room.* They are genuinely interested in your ideas and opinions, and it shows.

2. **Likeable**—They are warm, friendly, and sociable. They are open about their strengths and weaknesses as well as their successes and failures. They are comfortable in their own skin and aren't ashamed of their vulnerabilities.

3. **Confident**—They believe in themselves and others. They are upbeat and positive about the future. There is no doubt or hesitation in their delivery. They remain calm and composed in high-pressure situations. They focus on what they can control versus what they cannot.

Darlene, Sales Associate states,

"My manager has a great deal of personal power. He has a big personality and a great sense of humor. He's upbeat and positive, and generous with his time. I like being around him because he makes me feel special.

Managers and leaders with personal power are very strong in the areas of collaboration, empathy, fairness, open-mindedness, and networking. They make strong connections with people. They build alliances and coalitions across all departments and levels of the organization. They use their network to acquire information, gain support, and make needed connections to achieve their goals. The familiar saying, "It is not what you know but who you know," applies here.

USE YOUR POWER

Each manager has a unique combination of position, expertise, and personal power. The amount of power you possess will change as you get promotions, gain expertise, and increase your presence and interpersonal skills. It's important to use all the different types of power you possess. Ineffective managers don't use their power to their fullest potential.

INFLUENCING PEOPLE

A dictionary definition of *influence* suggests that it is when we change someone's attitude, beliefs, decisions, views, or we get them to do something we want done.

Courtesy of Paul B. Thornton

How do managers influence coworkers, customers, suppliers, etc.? They start by getting inside their circle—their world. What are their goals, needs, and frustrations? They ask questions to learn what people are thinking and feeling.

Effective managers tie the benefits of their ideas to the needs and goals of others. They explain what's in it for them—how they will benefit. Some of the tactics used by managers include:

► **Frame the Issue**—A frame around a picture tells us what to focus on. In a similar way, managers frame issues to get people to view the situation a certain way. Many charitable organizations try to get us to donate money by framing the problem in a way that appeals to our emotions.

► **Plant Seeds**—Managers are not able to influence someone on the first try. So they plant an idea and keep watering it until people see the value and accept the idea.

► **Bargain**—"If you do A, I'll do B." This is a common approach people use in business and in their personal lives.

► **Reciprocity**—"I did something for you last month, now it's your turn. You need to help me get my budget approved." Managers make people feel obligated by reminding them of how they helped them in the past.

► **Ingratiate**—Managers use sincere flattery and compliments to get people to be more open and receptive to their proposals.

► **Pressure**—Be aggressive. Wear people down. Keep asking for something over and over until the other person agrees.

► **Build Coalitions**—Recruit people that support their position. It's a more convincing argument to say, *"Eighty-five percent of the managers recommend . . ."*

► **Testimonials**—Solicit positive comments from other credible, high-profile people who will speak positively about your idea or accomplishment.

► **Set the Example**—Managers also influence people by what they do.

> "I am a big believer in the power of specific examples. I always provide real-world examples as to how my idea will help or improve the situation. People are more likely to buy into that idea when they can understand its benefits. I also need to demonstrate why I am passionate and fully committed to that idea."
>
> —Christine Phillips, Vice President–Operations, United Personnel

Managers use these tactics to influence people to support their ideas and get them to do certain things. But of course people aren't always convinced. Their reactions fall into three categories.

1. *Resistance*—People don't buy what the manager is selling.

2. *Compliance*—People go along with the manager's request but do the minimum. They do it with little energy and enthusiasm.

3. *Commitment*—People enthusiastically support the manager's request and take action with energy and passion.

Managers often face the additional challenge of influencing people over whom they have no direct managerial authority. Influencing others starts with the quality of the relationship managers have with others. In addition, no influence tactics will work if the person doesn't perceive some benefit to them. Managers should always consider the goals, needs, and expectations of the people they are trying to influence.

SUMMARY

Several things you need to remember . . .

- ▶ Managers need power to get things done.
- ▶ The more power you have, the more you can get done.
- ▶ If you have power, use it—put it to good use.
- ▶ Before you try to influence someone, find out what he or she is thinking and feeling.

DISCUSSION QUESTIONS

1. What type of power is the best to have? Why?

2. What is the fine line between using your power and abusing your power?

3. You've just been promoted to manager and you've developed a good rapport with most of your employees, but Kate Richardson and Owen Blake are always going to your supervisor with matters that should go through you. Both employees have been at the company for at least ten years longer than you have, and both know your supervisor very well. Explain how you will deal with this situation.

4. How would you go about trying to influence your boss to give you a pay raise?

Chapter 9

APPROACHES TO LEADING OTHERS

What is the right ratio of time spent managing versus leading?

What is the difference between a thought leader and a servant leader?

To succeed in today's business world, managers must also be leaders. As managers move <u>up</u> the organization, they spend more time leading and less time managing.

Leadership-guru Warren Bennis said, "Failing organizations are usually over-managed and under-led." Meaning the organization isn't changing fast enough to keep up with a changing world and marketplace.

▶ Managers use current methods, procedures, and processes to achieve established goals.

▶ Leaders focus on changing things for the better.

> "Leadership is lifting a person's vision to higher sights, the raising of a person's performance to a higher standard, the building of a personality beyond its normal limitations."
>
> —Peter Drucker

Effective leaders are never satisfied with the status quo. They believe that individuals, organizations, and even nations possess undiscovered talents and untapped resources. They seek to unleash the full potential of their followers, so they can reach higher and go farther than they previously thought possible.

LEADER TRAITS

Leaders come in all shapes and sizes. They don't all look and act the same. But all leaders possess the following three traits:

- ▶ **Confidence**—a strong belief in themselves and their followers.
- ▶ **Courage**—needed to take risks, challenge the status quo, and to speak up for their core beliefs and values.
- ▶ **Passion**—for their cause and vision.

THOUGHT LEADERS

They influence and inspire us by their ideas.

Thought leaders harness the power of their ideas to invoke change. They stretch people by helping them envision new possibilities. Teachers and professors introduce us to new concepts and models to understand things. At TED talks there are many professional thought-leaders who present cutting-edge ideas.

Transformational leaders offer up ideas that are game changers. Think: online shopping, digital photography, and UBER. A paradigm shift is a completely new and often radical way of viewing or doing things. Some ideas result in smaller, incremental changes. But all changes, whether big or small, start with a new idea.

For centuries, thought leaders have competed in the marketplace of ideas, using books, papers, and oral presentations. Today, they also use the Internet, social media, and other technological advances to disseminate their ideas more rapidly and broadly. E-books, blogs, e-zines, teleseminars, and webinars have made thought leadership instantaneously available to everyone.

Examples of thought leaders:

- ▶ Jack Welch—Many of his ideas challenged conventional business practices. Some of his leading-edge ideas included "workout and best practices," stretch goals, creating boundary-less organization (breaking down all "silos"), and pursuing six sigma quality.
- ▶ Walter "Walt" Disney was an American animator, film producer, director, and entrepreneur who dramatically influenced the field of entertainment. Along with his brother Roy O. Disney, he co-founded Walt Disney Productions, which today includes theme parks, movie production, and other entertainment venues. The corporation now has an annual revenue in excess of USD $55 billion. All of this came from Walt's ideas and imagination!
- ▶ Steven "Steve" Jobs was the co-founder, chairman, and CEO of Apple Inc., where he oversaw the development of the iMac, iTunes, iPod, iPhone, iPad, and numerous other innovations. He has been referred to as the "Father of the Digital Revolution," "a master of innovation," and "the master evangelist of the digital age."
- ▶ Dr. W. Edwards Deming was an American statistician, professor, author, lecturer, and consultant. After World War II, his ideas about quality and process control had a major positive impact and influence on Japanese manufacturing businesses. Subsequently, his concepts and teachings spurred a major quality revolution among American manufacturers and consumers.

Thought leaders attract followers and initiate change by the power of their ideas.

COURAGEOUS LEADERS

They influence and inspire us by their actions.

These types of leaders are the risk takers. They make bold moves that are visible for all to see. They influence people by speaking up and taking action in difficult situations. They have the courage to seek the truth, speak the truth, and venture into uncharted territories. President John Quincy Adams said, "If your actions inspire others to dream more, learn more, do more and become more, you are a leader."

In 2002, *Time* magazine selected Sherron Watkins (Enron), Coleen Rowley (FBI), and Cynthia Cooper (World-Com) as its featured "Persons of the Year." All three "whistleblowers" had the courage to confront higher-ups in their organizations, even though it meant jeopardizing their jobs and careers.

It takes courage to:

- ► Change the mission
- ► Question sacred cows
- ► Invest all your money in starting a business
- ► Set demanding goals
- ► Give candid feedback, and
- ► Fire poor performers.

Kevin Sharer, CEO of AMGEN, said,

"Leaders are trying to do something new. And new can be scary. It takes courage to put your ass on the line to make it happen. They are the risk takers who are willing to make the first move into unchartered territory. They take us to new and often unfamiliar places."

Examples of courageous leaders:

- ► Christopher Columbus was a fifteenth-century Italian explorer, navigator, and colonizer. His four voyages across the Atlantic Ocean led to general European awareness of the American continents. He had to exercise strong, courageous leadership to secure funding for his voyages, recruit crews, and venture into the unknown.
- ► Rosa Parks was an African American civil rights activist, whom the U.S. Congress called "the first lady of civil rights" and "the mother of the freedom movement." On December 1, 1955, in Montgomery, Alabama, she refused to obey the bus driver's order that she give up her seat to a white passenger. Her great courage marked a pivotal point in the Civil Rights Movement.
- ► Abraham Lincoln, the 16th president of the United States, served during the most difficult and dangerous period of our nation's history. Even though his life was constantly in danger and his policies were unpopular with many, he steadfastly held to his convictions and governed with strength, fairness, and dignity. On January 1, 1863, he courageously issued his memorable Emancipation Proclamation, which declared the freedom of slaves within the Confederacy.

Courageous leaders are powerful role models. They stand out by the decisive action they take.

INSPIRATIONAL LEADERS

They influence and inspire us by their passion.

They get people fired up! Inspirational leaders have great excitement and passion for their ideas and vision for the future. This type of leader knows how to tap into the larger purpose that energizes the human spirit. Their words touch our hearts and souls. Their passion is contagious.

Their optimism and encouragement make people feel good about themselves and the possibilities for a better future. They enlarge our ideas of who we are and what we can become.

Author and leadership guru, John Maxwell, said when you are passionate about something you're all-in. You spend endless hours thinking about the thing that drives you. This increases the depth of your knowledge and further strengthens your convictions.

Examples of inspirational leaders:

- ► Ronald Reagan, the 40th president of the United States, was known for his strong leadership on behalf of free enterprise and politically conservative ideals. In his second term, he presided over the end of the Cold War with the former Soviet Union. His inspirational leadership style incorporated excellent communication skills seasoned with humor and optimism.
- ► Martin Luther King, Jr. was an American clergyman, activist, and leader in the African American Civil Rights Movement. He is best known for his belief in nonviolent civil disobedience. His words and actions have inspired many people to speak up and stand up for what's right.
- ► Pat Summit was the leader of the University of Tennessee Lady Volunteers basketball program for thirty-eight years. She was known as an intense, demanding, focused, determined, and inspiring coach. She compiled a record of 1,098 wins and 208 losses, winning eight NCAA national championships, second only to the record ten titles won by UCLA men's coach John Wooden. Summit stands alone at the one thousand victories' plateau among all NCAA coaches.

Inspirational leaders attract followers and motivate people to change by the power of their passion and their strong convictions. They often create a sense of urgency by explaining the importance of timing and taking action now—not later.

SERVANT LEADERS

They influence and inspire us by the help they provide.

Former AT&T executive Robert K. Greenleaf popularized the concept of the servant leader in *The Servant as Leader*, an essay first published in 1970. Kent Keith, CEO of the Greenleaf Center for Servant Leadership, simplifies the concept by saying, "Servant leaders focus on identifying and meeting the needs of others rather than trying to acquire power, wealth, and fame for themselves." It's all about helping others succeed and prosper.

Max De Pree, former CEO of Herman Miller, said, "The first responsibility of a leader is to define reality. The last is to say thank you. In between, the leader is a servant."

Servant leaders help people and organizations achieve their potential. They ask questions and observe behavior to understand people's goals and what's holding them back. More specifically, servant leaders do three things:

1. **Ask questions** that help people clarify their goals and fine-tune their plan.

2. **Remove barriers** such as fears, obstacles, and self-limiting beliefs that can hold people back.

3. **Provide resources,** such as information, tools, time, budget, etc., in order to help people grow and develop.

They strive to foster an environment where employees are freed up and given the resources they need to do their best work.

Examples of servant leaders include:

▶ Mother Teresa founded the Missionaries of Charity, a Roman Catholic religious congregation, in Calcutta, India. Today, the ministry has more than 4,500 sisters ministering in 133 countries. The order runs hospices and homes for people with HIV/AIDS, leprosy, and tuberculosis; soup kitchens; children's and family counseling programs; orphanages; and schools. Members vow to give "wholehearted and free service to the poorest of the poor." Mother Teresa has received numerous honors, including the 1979 Nobel Peace Prize.

▶ Oprah Winfrey is the chairman of Harpo Inc. Her focus is helping others succeed. Many of her TV programs and outreach initiatives are aimed at removing obstacles, so people can achieve their potential. Her goal is to empower people to achieve their dreams.

▶ Max De Pree was the CEO of Herman Miller office furniture company from 1980 to 1987. His book *Leadership Is an Art* has sold more than 800,000 copies. Max states, "The first responsibility of a leader is to define reality. The last is to say 'thank you.' In between, the leader is a servant."

Servant leaders attract followers and motivate people to change by helping to remove obstacles that are in the way of their growth and development. They create a pass-it-on culture in which those who are helped then look to help others.

SUMMARY

Two things you need to remember . . .

▶ All leaders want to change the status quo for the better.

▶ There is more than one way to influence and inspire people to change.

DISCUSSION QUESTIONS

1. What is the fine line between too much enthusiasm and too little enthusiasm?

2. What is the fine line between providing too much service and too little service?

3. Do a search on the "Situational Leadership Model" that was developed by Paul Hersey and Ken Blanchard. Answer the following questions:

   a. What are the four styles mentioned in this model?

   b. What is the "best" style to use according to this model?

4. **CREATING CONSTRUCTIVE CONTROVERSY CASE STUDY**

   > Peter Esdale doesn't like to follow the crowd. He thinks groupthink is a common problem in many organizations. This former director of marketing for a consumer products company believes differences of opinion should be heard and appreciated. As Esdale states, "I have always believed I should speak for what I believe to be true."
   >
   > He demonstrated his belief in constructive controversy throughout his career. On one occasion, he was assigned to market Paul's spaghetti-sauce products. During the brand review, the company president said, "Our spaghetti sauce is losing out to price-cutting competitors. We need to cut our prices!"
   >
   > Peter found the courage to say he disagreed with the president. He then explained the product line needed more variety and a larger advertising budget. Prices should not be cut. The president accepted Esdale's reasoning. Later, his supervisor approached him and said, "I wanted to say that, but I just didn't have the courage to challenge the president."
   >
   > On another occasion, the president sent Esdale and sixteen other executives to a weeklong seminar on strategic planning. Esdale soon concluded the consultants were off base and going down the wrong path. Between sessions, most of the other executives indicated they didn't think the consultants were on the right path. The consultants heard about the dissent and dramatically asked participants whether they were in or out. Those who said "Out" had to leave immediately.
   >
   > As the consultants went around the room, every executive who privately grumbled about the session said "In." Esdale was fourth from last. When it was his turn, he said "Out" and left the room.

   a. What type of leader is Esdale?

   b. What would you have done if you were in his shoes?

Part IV

THE PROCESS

What is a process?

What's the difference between a product and a service?

What is a SMART goal?

What are the best ways to give an employee feedback?

When is it necessary to take disciplinary action?

What is the process managers need to follow to create and lead a high performing team?

Chapters 10 through 12 discuss the actions managers take to design, implement, and manage effective and efficient processes. A process is a set of defined steps taken to produce the desired result.

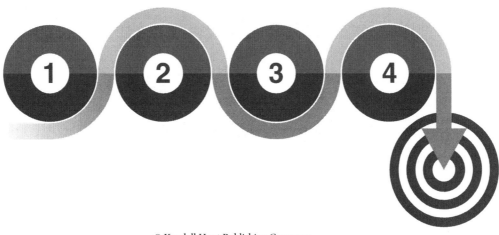

Chapter 10

MANAGING THE PROCESS

What are the characteristics of and effective and efficient process?

What is the difference between a process and a system?

In today's competitive environment managers must establish efficient processes. A process is a consistent, repeatable, step-by-step approach used to get something done. A business process involves some combination of materials, equipment, information, and people that produces a product or service.

- ▶ *Products* are tangible. You can see and touch them.
- ▶ *Service* relates more to the experience. How helpful and friendly was the person taking your order? How long did you have to wait before getting help?

Examples of business processes include:

- ▶ Interviewing candidates
- ▶ Paying bills
- ▶ Assembling parts
- ▶ Running meetings
- ▶ Resolving customer complaints

The three parts to a process include inputs, process steps, and outputs, as shown in the diagram below.

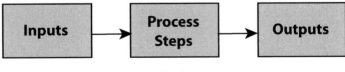

Courtesy of Paul B. Thornton

INPUTS

Inputs are the orders and requests from internal and external customers for products and services. Examples include:

- ► External customer—*"I'd like to order the shrimp dinner."*
- ► Internal customer—A manager says to the human resources director, *"I want to hire six software engineers. Get me some good resumes."*

Many positions within an organization require you to produce products and services (reports, plans, interviews, advice, recommendations) for other departments and groups within the business. These are your internal customers.

Inputs must be specific and clearly defined. Quantity requirements, quality standards, and due dates must be nailed down.

Some of the problems that can occur at the input step include:

- ► Some customers don't always know what they want or need. A former CIO for a large financial services company remembered, *"We often got an input from functional groups that were vague problems. They had a problem and they wanted us to solve it. We had to ask a lot of questions to identify the real need. You can waste a lot of time if you simply react to every request you receive."*
- ► Communication omissions and breakdowns—the person taking the order doesn't fully listen to the customer's input or misinterprets what the customer wants. Specific requirements (quality standards, due date, etc.) aren't stated or clearly defined.

If the order or input isn't clear, there's a high probability that the output—the product or service—will not be what the customer wanted.

Customers evaluate the input step by criteria such as:

- ► How easy or difficult was it to place the order?
- ► How long did it take for the person to take your order?
- ► How friendly, knowledgeable, and helpful was the person taking your order?

PROCESS STEPS

The "process steps" refers to all of the action steps required to produce the output. For example, the directions on the back of a cake mix box include the following:

1. Obtain ingredients, including cake mix, eggs, water, oil, and flour.
2. Preheat oven to 350°F.
3. Grease pans and dust with flour.

4. Blend in large bowl at low speed: cake mix, 3 egg whites, 1 cup water, and ¼ cup oil.

5. Beat 2 minutes at high speed.

6. Pour batter into pan.

7. Bake at 350°F for 40 minutes.

8. Cool cake in pan for 10 to 20 minutes.

9. Remove from pan.

Follow these nine steps and you will produce a cake. In a similar way, a work process can be broken down into a series of steps. Managers often use flowcharts to describe all of the steps and decisions made in a work process. Flowcharting is a useful tool because it provides a visual of what's going on from start to finish.

In some processes, such as education, counseling, and entertainment events, the customer participates in the process steps. For example, when working with a marriage counselor, the customer makes comments, answers questions, and contributes to the overall experience. In the case of education, the student must fully participate in the process to achieve the learning goals.

Some of the problems that occur related to the process steps include:

▶ The steps are not clearly defined.

▶ The steps are not followed.

▶ Employees don't know how to properly execute each step.

For any process to work well, the process steps must be known, understood, and followed. The amount of variation in the process steps will influence the amount of variation in the output. For example, if you use different ingredients, follow different steps, or leave out certain steps each time you bake a cake, the output (baked cakes) will vary significantly.

OUTPUTS

The output is the completed product or service and the payment of the item.

Customers evaluate the output by factors like the following:

▶ Did I get what I ordered?

▶ Product features—appearance, size, quality, functionality, warranty, cost, etc.

▶ Service experience—the attitude, knowledge, skills, and timeliness of the service provider

In many situations the customer is evaluating both the product quality and the service experience. For example, my wife and I recently dined at a local restaurant. Here's how I scored it:

▶ Product (food and drinks) —B+

▶ Service—C

MANAGING THE PROCESS

Managers manage multiple business processes in the department or function they work in. Effective managers manage their key processes so the products and services consistently meet or exceed customer expectations. Managing a process includes doing the following:

1. **Forecast Inputs**—Managers must estimate the number of orders they will be receiving for any process they are managing. This determines the required staffing levels. For example, a restaurant must forecast the number of customers who will be walking through the front door to determine staffing needs and inventory requirements.

2. **Document Steps**—Managers must define and document the steps in each of the key processes they manage.

3. **Train**—Employees must be educated and trained in how to perform each step.

4. **Measure**—Managers must determine what things to measure in each process. Some of the typical metrics that are kept include quantity, quality, cycle time, and cost.

5. **Customer Feedback**—Ongoing feedback from customers both formal and informal. Effective feedback helps managers and employees determine what changes are needed in the process.

Various quality gurus have stressed the importance of collecting data to understand and improve the performance of a process. Some of the individuals who have led this effort include:

▶ **W. Edwards Deming** is often referred to as the "father of quality control."

▶ **Joseph M. Juran** His book *Quality Control Handbook* describes his philosophy of quality control and quality management.

▶ **Philip B. Crosby** He developed the phrase "Do it right the first time" and the notion of *zero defects*, arguing that no amount of defects should be considered acceptable.

▶ **Kaoru Ishikawa** is best known for the development of quality tools called cause-and-effect diagrams, also called fishbone or Ishikawa diagrams.

Some of the tools they recommended to collect data to understand how a process is currently operating include:

▶ **Checklists**—These are lists of common defects related to a product or service. Each time a defect is observed the worker puts a checkmark in the appropriate box. It is a way of collecting data to identify when and where problems are occurring in the process. Checklists are a simple yet effective fact-finding tool that allows the worker to collect specific information regarding the defects observed.

▶ **Control Charts**—These charts are used to evaluate whether a process is operating within expectations relative to some measured value such as weight, width, or volume. For example, you could measure the weight of a sack of flour, the width of a tire, or the volume of a bottle of soft drink. When the production process is operating within expectation, it is said to be "in control."

▶ **Scatter Diagrams**—These graphs show how two variables are related to one another. They are particularly useful in detecting the amount of correlation, or the degree of linear relationship, between two variables.

► **Cause-and-Effect Diagrams**—These are used to help identify potential causes of specific quality problems. Specific causes of problems can be explored through brainstorming. The development of a cause-and-effect diagram requires the team to think through all the possible causes of a specific quality problem.

IMPROVING THE PROCESS

Customers are demanding. They want better quality, lower costs, and faster service. And the competition keeps improving. Competitive pressure requires organizations to constantly improve their key processes. Remember the words of Thomas Edison: "There is always a better way—find it." Companies with a *business as usual* culture don't last very long.

Some of the things managers can do to improve their process include:

1. **Observe customers** using your products. What issues or difficulties are they having? For example, L.L. Bean, which sells clothing and outdoor equipment, sends employees out to observe customers who are using the company's products. They may identify improvement opportunities just by observing customers.

2. **Study the "best in class" performers.** For example, what process do the very best bakeries use to produce their cakes? There are always new insights to be gained by studying top performers.

3. **Ask questions** about your current process.
    ► Does the physical layout of equipment facilitate the work?
    ► Does every step add value?
    ► Where are the bottlenecks or delays?
    ► Can we perform steps in parallel, rather than serially?
    ► Is there any equipment that would save time or reduce mistakes?
    ► Would new computer software, or training on existing software, help?

Process improvement is an ongoing, never-ending activity for both managers and employees. Managers must make every effort they can to simplify steps, eliminate unnecessary steps, and automate steps where appropriate. I have always liked and tried to follow this quote by French writer Antoine de Saint-Exupery: "Perfection is achieved, not when there is nothing more to add, but when there is nothing left to take away."

SYSTEMS

Managers at all levels need to understand the systems in their departments and organizations. A system is an organized collection of parts, processes, or subsystems that are integrated to accomplish an overall goal. Systems thinking is basically the ability to see the whole—the big picture—as well as all the parts of the whole. It involves taking a holistic perspective and understanding the interconnectedness of various parts.

For our purposes a system is the interaction between and among two or more processes. In the local, take-out pizza shop the four key processes include:

1. Taking orders

2. Cooking pizzas

3. Packaging orders

4. Delivering orders

The interaction of these processes is a system. All four processes must work together for the customer to get the desired pizza delivered at the promised time. The weakest link in any system will limit performance, and correcting the weak link will have a big payback in improved performance.

Systems like the human body have parts that are interdependent. The liver interacts with and affects other internal organs—the brain, heart, kidneys, etc. You can study the parts singly, but because of the interactions, it doesn't make much practical sense to stop there. Understanding of the system cannot depend on analysis alone. The key to understanding is, therefore, synthesis.

All processes must be aligned and integrated to make the overall system work effectively. In some situations, managers improve one process but the overall system doesn't improve. Managers need to see the big picture and understand how all the pieces fit together.

SUMMARY

Some things you need to remember . . .

► Business processes need to be effective and efficient.

► Improving key processes must be an ongoing priority.

► The overall system must be aligned and integrated.

DISCUSSION QUESTIONS

1. Do a Google search on W. Edwards Deming. What's his background? Which of his fourteen points for management do you think is most important? Why?

2. Construct a Pareto chart using the following data:

Causes of Customer Complaints	Frequency
Repair not completed on time	18
Repair cost exceeded estimate	25
Breakdown within two weeks	5
Car dirty upon pick-up	8
Repair people discourteous	10

3. How does the operation of the human body resemble a system?

Chapter 11

MANAGING PERFORMANCE

What is meant by a SMART goal?

What can managers do to help people perform at their best?

Managers work with and through people to get things done.

People are your most important asset. Every manager needs to help each of their employees to perform at their best each and every day. The steps involved in managing employees' performance are listed in the chart below.

The Performance Management Process

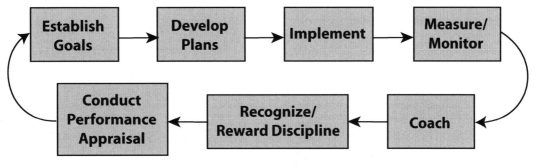

Courtesy of Paul B. Thornton

STEP 1: ESTABLISHING GOALS AND EXPECTATIONS

Employees need to know exactly what they are expected to accomplish. When establishing goals, managers need to remember the acronym SMART. Effective goals meet the following criteria:

- ▶ *Specific*—Pinpoint exactly what you want. *"Increase sales by 12 percent."* Vague goals like "improve quality" or "cut costs" are open to interpretation and can't be measured.
- ▶ *Measurable*—The more specific the goal, the easier it is to measure.

- *Accepted*—Goals must be accepted by those who have to achieve them. Employees must believe they have the skills and resources needed to achieve each goal.

- *Results oriented*—Focus on the desired outcome rather than process used to produce the product or service.

- *Time-bounded*—Specific dates and times provide focus and reduce confusion. *"Reduce costs by 7 percent by June 12th."* Goals without deadlines have a way of slipping away.

The general rule is to set goals that are challenging but attainable. If you have to set a stretch goal, you need to be able to justify why the significant increase is needed.

Managers can use any of the three management styles—directing, discussing, or delegating—to establish goals and expectations.

- **Directing**—*"Here is a list of your goals for the next three months."*

- **Discussing**—Ask questions and engage the employee on what needs to be accomplished. *"What sales goals should we set for the year?"*

- **Delegate**—*"I want you to identify your top seven goals for the next 12 months. Review your goals with me on Friday at 10:00 a.m."*

In general the more involved employees are in setting goals, the more committed they are to achieve them.

STEP 2: DEVELOP PLANS

Goals require plans. A plan is a roadmap to reach your goal. Start with your goal and work backward. Identify all the actions needed to go from point A to point G (goal achievement). Create a list of all action items and then determine who will do each task and the required time frames.

Managers can use any of the three management styles to create the plan.

- **Directing Style**—*"Here are the five steps you need to take to complete the XM-43 project by Friday."* If a manager wants something done a specific way, he needs to explain exactly how he wants it done.

- **Discussing Style**—*"What actions do you think are needed to increase sales by 20%?" "What can we do to reduce costs by 10%?"*

- **Delegating Style**—*"I want you to develop a plan to increase revenue by 12%. Let's get together Monday at 2:00 p.m. and review your plan."*

For more complex projects, plans need to identify the resources—people, money, and equipment—required to get the job done. We recently renovated our kitchen. My wife, Mary Jean, performed the role of project manager. Her plan included establishing a budget, selecting vendors, and ordering items such as appliances, cabinets, tile, and wallpaper. In addition, she had to coordinate and schedule electricians, painters, carpenters, and tile installers to do the work. The importance of *goal clarity* (exactly what needs to get done) and *role clarity* (who is responsible for what tasks) is critical. Things fall between the cracks when the plan is incomplete or lacking in specific details.

"My preferred style is to state the goal so it is clear. When developing the strategy I ask questions about the steps the individual thinks are necessary to achieve the goal. This approach creates individual ownership for the plan and the goal. Additionally, creating a strategy for implementation provides a roadmap that can be reviewed frequently to make sure that the person is staying on course."

— Alan Edington, Vice President of Operations, Tennessee Bun Company

Effective planning also involves anticipating problems and determining the actions you'll take to deal with them. Managers need to be flexible and react to changing circumstances. It's not just planning—once and done. Re-planning is often required as events unfold.

STEP 3: IMPLEMENT

Employees implement the plans. They take action to accomplish their goals. Implementation means doing the day-to-day work needed to produce the required products and services. The "to-do" list is the most basic level of implementation. This list includes items such as setting up meetings, returning phone calls, and analyzing data.

Mead Corporation has a 600-pound rock in their lobby. Steve Mason, Mead's CEO, explained the rock is a metaphor to remind people what it takes to move the rock. Meetings and planning sessions to discuss how to move the rock may be useful. But the rock doesn't move until someone implements the plan.

STEP 4: MEASURE AND MONITOR

Managers measure and monitor each employee's performance to determine if he or she is on track or not. Employees need to understand what's being measured and why it's important. There are two categories that managers need to focus on:

1. *What's getting done*—the output—the quantity and quality of the products and services being produced.

2. *How it's getting done*—this includes items such as attendance, attitude, effort, initiative, motivation, and teamwork. Are employees operating in accordance with the company values?

How often should managers measure and monitor an employee's performance: Daily? Weekly? Monthly? It depends on factors, such as the employee's skills and experience and the work they're doing. Also, when to monitor results relates to what makes sense in terms of key milestones.

Managers use the following approaches to measure and monitor employee performance.

▶ *Scheduled observations—"I'm going to sit in on your training program today."* Observe employees doing things such as running meetings, making sales calls, interviewing customers, and collaborating with coworkers.

- *Surprise visits*—Show up unannounced and observe what's happening or not happening. All military personnel have learned that after an order is given, the officer in charge needs to go out and see for himself whether it has been carried out.
- *Collect hard data*—Count the number of widgets produced, calls completed, or sales made. Use system generated data.
- *Reviews*—Budget reviews, written project summaries, and weekly reports are used to monitor what's getting done. *"What have you accomplished on the Harris proposal?"*

Managers need to make sufficient observations to identify patterns of behavior. Also, they need to be aware of these traps:

- Activity versus Results—Do not confuse activity (or effort) with results. Some employees are very busy . . . and while it looks like they are exerting a lot of energy, very little is actually getting accomplished.
- The Halo Effect—Just because an employee does one thing well, some managers generalize and conclude he is "outstanding" in all areas.
- The Horn Effect—The reverse. Just because an employee does one thing poorly, don't generalize and assume they are bad at everything.

STEP 5: COACH

It is important to make sufficient observations of an employee's behavior before determining what coaching is needed. The best managers are always looking for coaching opportunities to help employees sharpen their skills and add new skills to their toolbox.

Three points to consider before coaching are:

1. Does the employee understand the goals and expectations?
2. Does the employee know what success looks like?
3. Are there obstacles beyond the employee's control?

Managers can use any one of the three management styles to coach employees:

- **Directing Style**—You simply tell the person what he needs to do differently or what he needs to do more or less of. *"Noah, you need to establish your top three goals for this project by the end of this meeting." "Helen, you need to listen more and talk less in product review meetings."*
- **Discussing Style**—You ask questions that directly involve the individual in examining his or her own performance. Your questions help employees step back, reflect, and examine their performance. *"Joe, what's your critique of yesterday's meeting with our field service representatives?"* Also, discuss what actions the person thinks he needs to take to improve. *"Joe, what's one thing you think you could do to improve your sales presentations?"*
- **Delegating Style**—You ask the employee to do some self-coaching. *"Vera, I want you to reflect on today's conference. Identify three things you did well and three things you would do differently next year. Let's meet on Monday at 11:00 a.m. to discuss your observations."* When individuals coach themselves, they take responsibility for their own learning and personal growth.

It's useful to take advantage of "teachable moments." These are times when employees are most open to coaching and feedback. In some situations it is useful to ask the person, *"Are you open to some feedback on XYZ?"* Most employees will be curious and want to know what their manager thinks.

Someone succinctly described feedback as "information about past behavior, delivered in the present, which will hopefully influence future behavior." When giving feedback:

▶ **Focus on behavior.** Focus on what the employee said or did or didn't say or do. Don't exaggerate. State the facts. Provide specific examples. And let the employee give his point of view. Listen to his or her side of the story.

▶ **Explain the business consequences.** It's important the employee understand the business consequences of his or her current performance. The consequences of poor performance may be late deliveries, upset customers, disgruntled coworkers, poor quality, and lost sales.

▶ **Be timely.** After a problem is identified, generally the sooner feedback is given, the better. But it's also important to provide feedback when everyone is in an emotional state to hear (or share) the feedback.

▶ **Identify actionable steps.** It's important to define actionable steps the employee can take to improve. Ask the person to commit to taking specific steps by a certain date.

▶ **End with a summary.** At the end of the coaching or feedback session, ask the employee to summarize what has been discussed and agreed to.

▶ **Follow up.** Periodically check in with the employee to see what's being accomplished.

Each employee is unique. Learn what type of coaching and feedback works best for him or her.

STEP 6: RECOGNIZE/REWARD OR ADMINISTER DISCIPLINE

This step involves two very different and distinct actions depending on how the employee is performing.

Recognize and Reward

Author and consultant Ken Blanchard's motto is "Catch people doing something right." Recognizing and praising people is one of the most powerful tools managers have. When you recognize people, you're really saying, "I've noticed." Employees want to be noticed and to feel appreciated.

© Rawpixel.com/Shutterstock.com

Managers should be noticing and rewarding things like:

▶ Increased effort

▶ Better quality

▶ Faster response time

▶ Improved teamwork

Mother Teresa once said, "Kind words can be short and easy to speak, but their echoes are truly endless."

When recognizing and rewarding employees, managers should keep these points in mind:

▶ **Be timely.** The sooner you praise the employee after the good behavior, the better.

▶ **Be specific.** State exactly what the person did and how it helped.

▶ **Be sincere**. Show honest appreciation for what the person did.

Administering Discipline

It is an example of "tough love."

When an employee's performance continues to go downhill, managers need to step up and administer discipline. The objective of disciplinary action is to "formally" let the person know his performance is below expectations and it needs to improve immediately.

> "Discipline is the least favorite part of my job. However, it is necessary at times. When administering discipline, I explain the issue that occurred and how it is different than the expectation. Then I explain what needs to change for the employee to meet the expectation. Before finishing a disciplinary session, I ask for a commitment from the employee. The employee must buy into the change needed to improve performance."
>
> —Alan Edington, Vice President of Operations, Tennessee Bun Company

Most companies use progressive discipline, which typically involves the following four steps:

1. Verbal warning

2. Written warning

3. Final written warning or suspension

4. Discharge

However, the step you start at is determined by what the employee did.

When administering discipline, managers should use a directing style. As a matter of fact, the more direct and candid the manager is, the better. It often takes candid comments to wake the person up and break through their excuses and defenses.

When issuing a verbal or written warning, the following format is recommended:

1. State what the employee has done. *"You have been late six times and absent five times in the last month."*

2. State what you (the manager) have done. *"I have stressed the importance of you being here on time every day."*

3. State what you expect going forward. *"I expect you to be here at work every day and on time."*

4. State the consequences if improvement doesn't occur. *"If improvement doesn't occur, you are subject to further discipline up to and including discharge."*

After issuing a verbal warning, my rule of thumb is to observe the employee's performance over the next two to four weeks. If improvement doesn't occur, move to the next step and issue a written warning and so on. However, if the employee's performance improves it's important to recognize that improvement.

Managers need to review disciplinary actions with their human resources department. In addition, they need to keep accurate supervisory notes and document all actions taken.

STEP 7: CONDUCTING THE FORMAL PERFORMANCE APPRAISAL

At the end of a performance cycle, managers conduct a formal performance appraisal. If the manager has done an effective job of coaching and providing feedback throughout the year, the employee's overall performance rating will not be a big surprise. It's important to keep good notes documenting examples of each employee's strengths and areas needing improvement.

> "We complete two performance appraisals annually—a mid-year and an end of year. I establish goals for both of these timeframes and indicate if a 'new goal' is required. I use a directing or delegating style when establishing goals. However with special projects—I use a discussing style. I believe in 'special projects.' I like to discuss opportunities for team members to take on a new initiative that will help the department or company."
>
> —Kate Labor, Vice President, Customer Service, Systems and Software, Division of Harris Corporation

When managers schedule and prepare to conduct a performance appraisal they should consider the following points:

1. Select a location that is comfortable and free of distractions.

2. Schedule the review and notify the employee at least five days in advance.

3. Ask the employee to prepare for the session by reviewing his performance and key accomplishments. This could include having the employee do a <u>self-assessment</u> by filling out the performance appraisal form.

4. Review the performance documentation you have collected throughout the year. Concentrate on the performance patterns that have occurred.

5. Complete the performance appraisal form.

Conducting the Appraisal

Managers can use each of the three management styles when conducting the performance appraisal.

▶ **Directing Style**—For some points on the appraisal you may want to be direct and tell the employee exactly what he did well and where he needs to improve. Always be prepared to give specific examples.

▶ **Discussing Style**—There are some topics you will want to discuss. Ask questions and listen to the employee's view of his performance. Be open and willing to change your evaluation if necessary.

▶ **Delegating Style**—There may be some items where you want the employee to go off on their own and create an action plan for improvement.

Spend most of the time focusing on the employee's strengths and positive contributions. But remember that you must also cover opportunities for improvement. Also, ask the employee in what ways you can improve as a manager. What can you do to help the employee perform at a higher level?

Once the appraisal is completed, you should provide a copy of the appraisal to the employee and to the human resources department.

SUMMARY

Some things you need to remember . . .

▶ Set goals that are specific and time-bounded.

▶ Monitor progress; identify patterns of behavior.

▶ Provide caching and feedback as needed.

▶ Recognize good and improved performance.

▶ Help people grow and develop.

DISCUSSION QUESTIONS

1. **SETTING EXPECTATIONS CASE STUDY**

   > You are the newly appointed store manager of a Grocery Superstore. There are thirty-six full-time and forty-two part-time employees. All stores in the chain have been pressured to achieve aggressive profit targets. The former store manager achieved his financial goals. However, he fell far short in the store's safety performance. You are expected to do much better.
   >
   > Last year, the store accident rate was twice that of other stores in the chain: twenty-eight injuries—nine of which resulted in lost workdays.
   >
   > The Deli & Bakery Manager had fourteen injuries; five of which resulted in lost workdays. These involved cuts, burns, slips, and falls. Several burns occurred in the bakery area. In addition, three baggers sustained a fall in the parking lot while riding their empty grocery carts, which is a clear violation of policy. The most serious injury occurred when a janitor left puddles of wax in an aisle and failed to put up warning signs. This resulted in two serious accidents. Another employee slipped on a wet floor and fell, injuring his left leg and head.
   >
   > As new store manager, you are expected to immediately address the safety issue with your employees.
   >
   > As store manager, what goal would you set for the Deli and Bakery Manager regarding accidents and injuries?

2. *"Your goal is to increase productivity by 12 percent. I know you have lost several people but see what you can do."*

   What's wrong this goal statement?

3. At what point can a person's strength become a weakness?

4. Indicate whether each statement is "true" or "false." If the statement is false, rewrite it as a true statement.

   a. Managers should always be looking for opportunities for others to improve.

   b. The test of helping effectiveness is whether an employee's performance improves.

   c. Once an employee has mastered a task satisfactorily, your coaching job is finished.

   d. If managers want others to behave in certain ways, they need to model the behavior.

   e. It's preferable to let others come up with their own ways to improve rather than to provide solutions for them.

   f. Feedback tells people how well they're progressing toward their goals.

   g. Negative feedback is more likely to be accepted when combined with positive feedback.

   h. Objective negative feedback is more likely to be accepted than the subjective variety.

   i. Specific feedback is more effective than general feedback.

j. Delays between a recipient's undesirable behavior and providing feedback on that behavior should be avoided.

k. Don't give criticism unless it is desired by the recipient.

5. A manager gave this feedback to his employees. Recommend ways the manager could be more effective when giving feedback.

    "Barb, you're just not doing the kind of work I would expect of you. I realize you're a woman and all, but you took this job. So you need to crank it up and do as well as the guys."

6. How can a manager deliver a strong negative message in a way that gets the point across while preserving the relationship?

7. Prepare a written warning using the format described in this chapter. Your employee, Fred Harris, has the following attendance record:

    ▶ November: Absent 2, Late 4

    ▶ December: Absent 3, Late 4

    ▶ *January 4—Issued Verbal Warning*

    ▶ January: Absent 3, Late 3

    ▶ February: Absent 2, Late 2

Chapter 12

CREATING, MANAGING, AND LEADING TEAMS

What are the stages of team development?

A team is a small number of people who are committed to working together to achieve the desired goal. With teams, there is *interdependence* between and among team members. Team members work together, which includes talking, sharing ideas, debating issues, collaborating, establishing goals, making decisions, and dealing with changing priorities.

Most research indicates the ideal number of people to have on a work team is between five and twelve. But of course, the nature of the task influences the size of the team.

High performing teams have these things in common:

1. An effective team leader

2. Talented and motivated team members

3. Effective and efficient team processes

TEAM LEADER

The team leader plays a major role in the success of any team. The best team leaders have three important skills.

1. *Task Skills* include the ability to set goals, establish priorities, assign roles and responsibilities, plan and run effective meetings, and monitor results.

2. *People Skills* include the ability to build relationships, connect with people, resolve conflicts, motivate, and celebrate success.

3. *Diagnostic Skills* include the ability to diagnose what individuals or the whole team needs to move forward.

Effective team leaders know when to use the directing, discussing, and delegating management/leadership styles.

TEAM MEMBERS

You want people who meet the following criteria:

- ▸ Have the knowledge and skills to excel at performing their assigned role
- ▸ Highly motivated and interested in the problem or opportunity
- ▸ Team players—committed to supporting and helping each other

In his talks, articles, and books, author and speaker Jim Collins has made the following point: you need to get the right people on the bus and the wrong people off the bus.

© Kendall Hunt Publishing Company

Do you want a diverse group of people in terms of experiences, sex, ages, education, work history, thinking styles, etc.? It depends on the problem or opportunity the team is pursuing. In some cases you want diversity. In other cases it may not be needed. A cross-functional team is desirable when you are dealing with major initiatives that impact the total organization.

It's helpful to have people who can perform various roles, including:

- ▸ **Strategic Thinker**—someone who sees the big picture and connects the dots at a high level
- ▸ **Detail Oriented**—someone who's able to identify all the relevant details needed to get the job done
- ▸ **Facilitator**—someone who will engage people and help the team stay on track and follow a logical process
- ▸ **Relationship Oriented**—someone who is able to gauge how team members are feeling and knows how to build and strengthen relationships
- ▸ **Driver**—someone who keeps the team moving forward to accomplish the desired goal

TEAM PROCESSES

Top teams are effective and efficient at communicating, making decisions, and running meetings.

© ESB Essentials/Shutterstock.com

Communicating

Good communication is vital for team success. This requires a foundation of trust and openness to all ideas and points of view. Some of the communication rules that team members embrace and practice include:

- ▶ Speak up. Say what's on your mind
- ▶ Be respectful
- ▶ Criticize ideas; not people
- ▶ Listen and fully consider all ideas

"I have learned that teams fail due to a lack of openness more than anything else. I want each team member to feel safe in stating his or her opinion. At the same time, I want them to be open to other points of view and to question their own personal assumptions by asking: 'In what way could my assumptions be wrong?' As a team leader, I try to model being 'open' to all points of view. It's important to be cognizant when people start to get defensive."

—Kevin McManus, Plant Manager, DaVinci Gourmet

Making Decisions

Teams need to make timely decisions about goals, plans, assignments, etc. Some of the decision-making rules members embrace and practice include:

- ▶ Strive to reach consensus
- ▶ Avoid analysis paralysis
- ▶ Disagree and commit

> At Intel, Andy Grove demanded that his people argue and debate the issue, but once a decision is made they should fully support the decision. He originated the phrase "disagree and commit."

Running Meetings

Teams spend a lot of time in meetings. Some of the meeting management rules members embrace and practice include:

- ▶ Start and end meetings on time
- ▶ Always have an agenda
- ▶ Everyone contributes
- ▶ Put cell phones away

Holding People Accountable

Some of the rules related to holding people accountable that team members embrace and practice include:

- ▶ Have clearly defined goals and deadlines.
- ▶ All team members hold each other accountable for assigned tasks.
- ▶ No surprises. If you are going to have difficulty meeting a deadline, ask for help.

STAGES OF TEAM DEVELOPMENT

Teams, like personal relationships, go through stages. Teams don't become great teams overnight. It takes time for team members to develop trust, learn to collaborate, and understand each other's thinking styles and behavior patterns.

Psychologist B. W. Tuckman originally conducted research on small group interactions and described four stages of team evolution—forming, storming, norming, and performing. Each stage includes new challenges and opportunities to resolve issues, build relationships, and clarify roles. This model was first proposed in 1965. In 1977, Tuckman, jointly with Mary Ann Jensen, added the adjourning stage. The diagram on the following page shows the five stages.

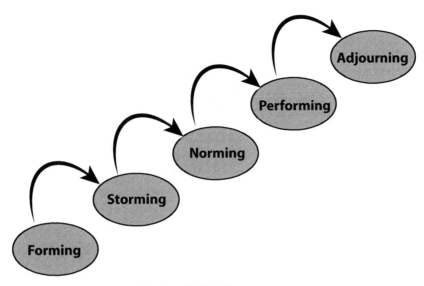

Courtesy of Paul B. Thornton

While it may look as if teams go through these stages in a neat and orderly progression, they don't. They bounce back and forth, as members leave, new people join, and the team experiences major successes and setbacks. It's often two steps forward and one step back.

There are certain issues and opportunities that arise in each of the stages. The team leader needs to take specific actions to help the team members work through these issues and continue to make progress.

FORMING STAGE

In the forming stage, team members meet for the first time. They communicate in a polite, tentative manner. Extroverts dominate conversation. Little, if any conflict exists. Team members form impressions about their colleagues' personalities, work habits, and motivation.

In the forming stage, people have questions like:

- ▶ Why was I selected for this team?
- ▶ How much time and effort will this require?
- ▶ What's in it for me? What can I learn?
- ▶ Who are these other people and why were they selected?

Actions Team Leaders Can Take

The Task

- ▶ Clearly define the task—exactly what needs to be accomplished.
- ▶ Establish goals and priorities.
- ▶ Define roles and responsibilities.

The People

- ▶ Explain how and why team members were selected.
- ▶ Discuss what's in it for the team members. Explain how they will benefit.
- ▶ Give team members a chance to get to know each other.

Team Processes

- ▶ Establish operating rules—determine how the team will work together.

STORMING STAGE

It's difficult for team members to consistently work together in a highly productive manner. Hidden agendas, hurt feelings, and interpersonal conflicts often develop. Arguments and differences in work styles arise. The conflicts may be about goals, priorities, roles, and responsibilities. Some team members may not agree with their role or feel their ideas aren't being considered.

Team members look for support and ask themselves questions such as:

- ▶ Who agrees with my point of view?
- ▶ Who are my allies?
- ▶ What can I do to gain more power and influence?

The storming stage is often marked by power struggles. Team members align with others who see things the way they do. Subgroups may develop. Each subgroup may have opposing goals, priorities, and strategies.

Team members need to learn how to work through conflicts and find productive ways to disagree, negotiate, collaborate, and work together. Conflict isn't bad but it must be handled in a professional and productive manner. Mishandled conflict can create hurt feelings, lack of trust, and disengagement.

Actions Team Leaders Can Take

The Task

- ▶ Remind all team members of the overall team's goals.

The People

- ▶ Address issues early on—when they arise.
- ▶ Help team members understand and appreciate their similarities and differences.

Team Processes

- ▶ Reinforce operating rules. "*We agreed to attack issues not people.*"
- ▶ If necessary, establish additional rules of engagement regarding conflicts.

The honeymoon is over. Team leaders need to help individuals find common ground and learn to argue in a professional way.

NORMING STAGE

Having worked through conflicts and disagreements, team members now understand each other better and appreciate each other's knowledge, skills, and experience. Team members become more interdependent. Team members discover there are many benefits to working together.

Team leaders and team members need to be aware of the evolving norms related to the task, the people and the processes the team is using. Do the norms align with the agreed upon operating rules? Some norms will be in alignment, and some may not be.

- ▶ *"We agreed to start meetings on time. We've fallen into the habit of people showing up five to ten minutes late."*
- ▶ *"We agreed to be open and honest, yet some people are withholding their true feelings."*
- ▶ *"We agreed to hold each other accountable. Are we doing that?"*

Team leaders need to be aware of the evolving norms and make sure they are aligned with the team's values and operating rules.

Actions Team Leaders Can Take

1. Set the example. Model the desired behaviors.
2. Discuss the evolving norms.
3. Point out differences between norms and operating principles.

Norms are important. They establish the framework that influences how team members work together and the quality of what they produce.

PERFORMING STAGE

All team members are fully engaged—participating, collaborating, and achieving great results. The team is performing at a high level. Team members understand and accept their roles and responsibilities. Team members are able to openly discuss ideas and resolve disagreements on their own. They learn quickly and are committed to continuous improvement.

Teams are described as being highly efficient and effective.

- ▶ *Efficient*—no waste. Team members use their expertise, time, and other resources in the most productive way
- ▶ *Effective* —they are focused on the right things

Here's a quote from a winning football team that exemplifies the performing stage:

> "...We had energy out there and we were feeding off each other. Players listen to coaches; coaches listen to players. Players listen to each other. Each player executed his part of the overall plan. We trusted each other. It was a special day!"

"Nothing succeeds like success!" As teams become more successful, team members become more committed to each other and the team's goals. Team cohesiveness increases when members work together and achieve success.

Actions Team Leaders Can Take

1. Celebrate success. Point out not only what the team is accomplishing but also how they are working together.

2. Don't let the team get complacent. Find new ways to challenge individual team members and the team as a whole to perform at a higher level.

3. Delegate more responsibility to the team.

ADJOURNING STAGE

The team has completed their assignment, and now the team is being broken up. Team members may experience a range of emotions including pride (of accomplishment), relief (the project is done), sadness (will no longer be working with these people), and anxiety (what's my next assignment).

Actions Team Leaders Can Take

1. Reward and recognize individual and team accomplishments.

2. Capture lessons learned.

3. Conduct a closure ceremony. Review the team's task and key accomplishments, and say goodbye to all team members.

This allows all team members to fully understand what they accomplished and how they did it. It provides a sense of closure before people move on to new projects.

SUMMARY

Several things manager/leaders of team need to remember . . .

▶ The task must be precisely defined and clearly understood.

▶ Get the right people on the bus and the wrong people off the bus.

▶ Effective team processes must be established.

▶ Help the team advance through various stages.

DISCUSSION QUESTIONS

1. Go to YouTube and watch the video "The Five Dysfunctions of a Team," featuring Patrick Lincioni.

   a. What are the five dysfunctions he discusses?

   b. In your experience, what is the major cause of a team not functioning effectively?

2. Think of a time when you were on a high performing, very successful team. In your opinion what made the team so successful?

   a. What made it a great team?

   b. What traits/characteristics did the team leader possess?

   c. What was the team's operating rules?

3. Interview the coach of a high school, college, or professional team. Discuss the following:

   a. How does he/she define teamwork?

   b. How does he/she deal with conflict between players?

   c. What does he/she think is the most important responsibility of a team leader?

4. Your team has progressed into the storming stage. A struggle for control has emerged between two strong members. If one suggests an idea, the other immediately rejects it. Between team meetings, they are both spending time trying to elicit support of other team members for their cause. The rest of the team is becoming uncomfortable. Meetings are becoming strained.

   a. If you were the team leader, what would you do?

5. **REMOTE CONTROLS CASE STUDY**

   > You manage four teams, which includes forty-eight employees. One of your teams is the twelve-person Remote Control Assembly Team. You recently hired Ted Thomas because he appeared to be smart, highly motivated, and a team player. He's done assembly work for the past three years.
   >
   > Each member of the Remote Control Assembly Team is responsible for assembling and testing a variety of remote controls for TVs, garage doors, and music systems. As a way of creating healthy competition among the team members, you have been recording each member's daily production output and posting it in the team's work area. At the end of each week, the team member who has assembled the most remote controls without a quality failure receives a $75 bonus. Several different team members have won the $75 bonus. However, overall production numbers aren't increasing.
   >
   > Ted joined the Remote Control Assembly Team two weeks ago. His first week was primarily training. This week Ted has a workstation in the assembly area. Ted is a quick learner and understands the business need for producing both quality and quantity. He likes competition and believes he can win the $75 bonus on a regular basis.

During the hiring interview, he said that with having a wife and three kids, every bit of extra money helps. You recently asked Ted how things were going. According to Ted, two of his teammates cornered him in the cafeteria during lunch. They told him that under no circumstances was he to assemble more than 225 remote controls a day. One of the employees said, "We all work at a comfortable pace around here. If you assemble more than 225 remotes a day, then we'll have to." Ted went on to say that the second employee told him, "And by the way, no one gets to win the weekly production award until they've been around for at least six months . . . so wait your turn."

a.   Is the Remote Control Assembly Team really a team?

b.   What should the team leader do?

c.   What should Ted do?

Part V

MANAGEMENT SKILLS

What can managers do to effectively and efficiently manage their time?

What is the appropriate ratio of talking versus listening for a first-line manager?

What can managers do to improve their communication skills?

What does it take to deliver a great presentation?

What are the ingredients of an effective interview?

What skills do managers need to make the best decisions?

What's the best way to motivate employees?

Chapters 13 through 24 will help answer these questions.

Managers need a set of strong skills to manage their people and their key processes. They must be efficient and effective at managing their time; communicating in multiple ways; defining and solving problems; dealing with difficult people; and managing their stress. Every day, managers use a wide range of skills.

Great Management Skills

© liravega/Shutterstock.com

Chapter 13

MANAGING TIME

What does it take to effectively and efficiently manage your time?

Celebrated Management Consultant Peter F. Drucker once said,

"Everything requires time. It is the only truly universal condition. All work takes place in time and uses up time. Yet most people take for granted this unique, irreplaceable, and necessary resource. Nothing else, perhaps, distinguishes effective executives as much as their tender loving care of time."

New managers often find it very difficult and challenging to manage their time. They often feel overwhelmed for a variety of factors including:

- ► New tasks keep landing on their desk
- ► More meetings to plan, conduct, and attend
- ► More papers and reports to read
- ► Increased e-mails to respond to
- ► Coworkers and employees interrupt with problems and questions

So what's the answer? Every manager must learn how to <u>effectively</u> and <u>efficiently</u> manage their time.

EFFECTIVE TIME MANAGEMENT

Remember, being effective means being focused on the right things. When it comes to time management, being effective means you are using your time wisely. You must focus on the right goals and the right priorities.

Vincent Maniaci, President of American International College said,

> "Some of the best advice I ever received came from Dr. Jay McGowan, President, Bellarmine University. He told me that you may think you have 10 things to focus on, but you really only have one or maybe two, and three at the most. The big question—are you focused on the right things."

Managers need to be clear on their top priorities.

Remember the 20/80 rule. Separate the "vital few" from the "trivial many." In his book, *Keep it Simple*, Joe Calloway states,

> "When we are focused on what is most important, we no longer have to wade through the endless sea of choices that can stretch before us. We make better decisions. We become more effective. We experience less stress. Getting focused is the path to simplicity, and simplicity is the path to success and fulfillment."

The best managers know both what is important and to stay focused on those important things.

© Stuart Miles/Shutterstock.com

Here are some actions you can take to stay focused:

1. **Write down your top goals and priorities.** Make them visible. Some managers post their goals in their office. Entrepreneur and motivational speaker Jim Rohm maintains that the key to time management is just staying in charge. To stay in charge, keep a written set of goals with you at all times and review them several times a day.

2. **Learn to say "No," but do so in a nice way.** Don't over-obligate yourself. Some requests you receive aren't relevant to your core job responsibilities and your top priorities. *"I have to say 'no.' I have several other tasks I need to complete by Friday."*

   Keep these words from Warren Buffet in mind. *"The difference between successful people and very successful people is that very successful people say 'no' to almost everything."*

3. **Minimize interruptions.** Phone calls, hallway conversations, colleagues stopping by your office—all of these can interrupt your focus and ability to get things done. Let people know when you are available, and when you are not. It may be appropriate to find a location that is free of distractions that you can use as needed.

EFFICIENT TIME MANAGEMENT

Efficiency means "no waste." The best managers don't waste their own time or that of their employees.

Obviously, wasting time is not productive. Some of the ways managers waste their time include:

1. Attending unproductive meetings

2. Being disorganized

3. Not delegating

4. Being a perfectionist

5. Using one hundred words to make your point when ten would have been sufficient

6. Establishing vague goals, muddy expectations, and unclear agreements

7. Procrastinating

8. Worrying excessively about things you can't change

Here are some things you can do to use your time efficiently:

1. **Create a "to-do" list.** Get in the habit of creating a daily to-do list. Start by listing all of your goals for the day. Identify the next actions you need to take to make progress in accomplishing your goals. Break down tasks to the smallest possible action you can take. Once your list is complete, mark each item as "A"—high priority, "B"—medium, or "C"—low. Needless to say, start by focusing on your As.

2. **Get organized.** Use a paper or electronic calendar to schedule meetings, appointments, and reminders of due dates. Keep it as simple or detailed as you feel appropriate. Also, establish a filing system as needed for both paper and electronic documents.

3. **Handle each piece of paper or electronic document only once.** For example, if you pick up a piece of paper, don't just move it to a new location on your desk—take action! Remember, there are only three things you can do with a piece of paper or an electronic document:

   ▶ File it.

   ▶ Throw it away or delete it.

   ▶ Take action.

4. **Keep Track.** You need a system to know who is assigned what tasks and when they're due. Create folders (either paper or electronic) for your projects so that you can track assignments and due dates.

5. **Delegate.** Effective delegation can free up time. Always consider if it makes sense to assign the task to someone else. Each day take a look at your to-do list and consider what you can delegate. You may be able to delegate some things to your boss, colleagues, and/or your direct reports.

6. **Read appropriately.** You don't necessarily need to read every word of every article, memo, and report. Determine the priority of the reading material you receive. In some cases all you need to do is skim the material for the major points. In other cases you need to read every word very carefully.

7. **Reduce the amount of time you spend procrastinating.** We all procrastinate to some extent. Break big tasks down into bite-size pieces. Set deadlines to begin working on certain tasks. Remember that getting started often creates momentum to continue. When you catch yourself procrastinating, ask yourself: "What am I avoiding?"

8. **Lead productive meetings.** A lot of time is wasted in unproductive meetings. If you are running the meeting, make sure you have a clear purpose and agenda with time frames. If you are attending a meeting, make sure there is a specific and compelling reason for you to be there.

9. **Periodically identify what you can stop doing.** There may be some things you are doing that don't add value, such as unnecessary paperwork or unneeded meetings. Eliminating tasks and activities will free up a lot of time to pursue other priorities. Continually look for things you can stop doing.

10. **Post reminders in your work area.** Some managers post a word or phrase like, "Do it now!" or, "Handle paperwork once!" as reminders to stay productive.

SUMMARY

Some things you need to remember . . .

▶ Time is a limited resource.

▶ Effective time management starts with knowing your goals and priorities.

▶ Efficient time management starts with identifying time wasters and then taking steps to eliminate them.

DISCUSSION QUESTIONS

1. What is your biggest time management challenge?

IN-BASKET EXERCISE—GOURMET HOT DOGS

The Situation

It is Tuesday and you are just returning from an extended weekend stay at the beach. You are the Northeast regional manager for a national fast-food merchandiser specializing in a limited menu, high quality products and services. Your office is in Springfield, Massachusetts. You're responsible for sales and profits.

Resources include sixteen hot dog carts that sell gourmet hot dogs with unique toppings, soda, and chips. The hot dog carts are located in Hartford, Boston, Springfield, Worcester, and Providence. Each hot dog cart has one operator. Each operator has a cell phone and a laptop computer.

Assignment

Review your voice mail, e-mail, and other events confronting you on Tuesday at the start of your workday. For each item, indicate the following:

- ▶ The priority (high, medium, or low)
- ▶ Your response—What would you say or do?
- ▶ Your method of responding (phone, e-mail, letter, etc.)
- ▶ Briefly explain your thought process.

Voice mail messages from:

1. <u>Your boss:</u> "... and as a result, I need you at Corporate New York City on Friday for a 10:00 a.m. meeting to review and discuss new models for capturing a larger share of the fast-food market ..."

2. <u>Al, unit 7 leader (Boston):</u> "Just want you to know I've been given an offer by another chain that looks pretty good. Anything you can do to get me to stay? I like the company and money isn't everything!"

3. <u>Your hot dog supplier:</u> "Our packaging vendor unexpectedly closed its doors and we'll be unable to deliver product to your locations for 24 hours. We apologize profusely."

4. <u>Mary, unit 2 leader (Hartford):</u> "With the convention that will be in town next week, we should see a nice increase in sales. You might want to swing by and see how things are going."

E-mail messages from:

1. <u>National Restaurant Association:</u> "... and as a reminder, our national convention is coming up in eight weeks. If you haven't already made your hotel reservations, we suggest you do so soon since space is at a premium."

2. <u>A peer in another region:</u> "I understand you've come up with a new process for keeping topping dispensers free of blockages. Any chance you can give me some help in bringing my units up to speed?"

3. <u>Your VP of finance:</u> "I didn't get your budget projections that were due Friday—must have by noon Tuesday."

4. <u>Your dentist:</u> "Reminder: we look forward to seeing you on Friday at 10:00 a.m. for your periodic checkup."

5. <u>Your CEO</u>—Memorandum to all supervisors: "As you know, our sales are flat. Wall Street is not responding to our continuing efforts, although successful, to cut costs and grow margins. Somehow, we must reinvent ourselves and overcome the roadblocks that seem to be getting in the way of our breaking out to a new level of performance. I need your help and would be interested in your thoughts as to how we might position the company for significantly greater returns. . . ."

Other events shortly after your arrival:

1. <u>Your HR rep</u> interrupts your train of thought, saying, "I need ten minutes to bring you up to speed on a potential breach of company policy by one of your unit leaders."

2. <u>Your administrative assistant</u>, obviously ailing from a persistent case of the flu, approaches you and announces that it would be in everyone's best interest if she were to return home and get plenty of rest. She will not be in tomorrow but hopes to be back by Friday.

3. <u>Your boss</u> calls and states, "I've heard some great things about Al (unit 7 leader). He's doing a super job. Please tell him to keep up the good work."

FROZEN FOODS CASE STUDY

Jan is the vice president of sales and marketing for a frozen food company. She has twelve sales representatives and two marketing managers (Irene and Chris) reporting to her. The company sells frozen food items to grocery store chains, such as Stop & Shop, and some restaurants. Jan was hired a year ago to energize the sales organization and refocus the marketing department. She is eager to "make her mark" and impress the president who hired her.

Irene is responsible for creating product brochures and fliers that describe quarterly promotions. In addition, she recently coordinated a semi-annual sales conference for approximately sixty people. She also assisted six of the sales reps on price quotes, coordinating information on deliveries and resolving problems such as customers who received damaged goods. Irene is very good at her job and has consistently received "excellent" performance ratings from her previous boss.

On Tuesday, April 6, Irene received an e-mail from Jan, assigning her eighteen action items. There were no due dates or priority indications given for any of the action items. Irene sent an e-mail back to her boss, asking which of these action items had the highest priority and due dates. Jan responded, "They're all important, but I suppose numbers 3, 7, 11, and 12 are the most important."

Irene immediately began working on these four items, in addition to her daily responsibilities. On Thursday, April 8, Irene received another e-mail from her boss, listing another seven action items. Again, there were no due dates or priority assigned.

Irene worked very late on Friday and all day Saturday on items 3 and 7 from the first e-mail. At 9:00 a.m. on Monday, she handed her boss a three-page report that addressed item 3 and a one-page recommendation that addressed item 7. Jan responded, "These items really aren't that important. I really need the sales data from the first quarter (item 11). Do you have that data? I'm leaving on a four-day business trip. Can you have the data for me by noon?" Irene, now frustrated, replied, "I'll try my best."

Irene got back to her desk and thought to herself, "My voice mail and e-mail are just going to have to wait." Unbeknownst to her, she had six phone messages from sales reps. Irene scrambled to pull together the sales data and gave it to her boss just as she was leaving the building. Irene didn't have time to proofread and check some of the numbers, which left her with a knot in her stomach. She was quite concerned about the quality of her work and didn't like "rush jobs" like this.

On Wednesday, Irene received that dreaded e-mail from her boss, which read as follows:

> "This sales data you summarized seems to be missing information from the Boston area. Are you sure these numbers are accurate?"

In addition, the e-mail listed nine new action items. A second e-mail (from one of the sales reps she supports) said, "Irene, what's going on? I asked you four days ago for a simple quote and you haven't gotten back to me yet. I need it ASAP."

1. What recommendations do you have for Jan?

2. What recommendations do you have for Irene?

Chapter 14

SENDING AND RECEIVING MESSAGES

What is your ratio of sending messages (talking) versus receiving messages (listening)?

How often are you involved in communication breakdowns?

Managers spend a great deal of time communicating with customers, bosses, employees, peers, and vendors. Many managers spend between 70–90 percent of their time speaking and listening. All managers and leaders must be able to communicate their ideas clearly, concisely, and completely. In addition, they need to be good listeners. Top managers spend as much time listening as they do talking. Having the ability to communicate both effectively and efficiently is one of the most important skills managers must possess.

EFFECTIVE COMMUNICATIONS

Effective managers send the right messages to the right people at the right time. In addition, they ask the right questions and listen intently to people's answers. They initiate and participate in the right conversations. An effective message is relevant to the manager's goals and priorities.

Ineffective managers send messages that miss the mark for various reasons, including:

- ► Lack of focus
- ► The tone of the message is inappropriate. Some managers lacking in emotional intelligence can come across as angry and uncaring.
- ► Unwilling to deliver a difficult message
- ► Wrong level—too general or too much detail

EFFICIENT COMMUNICATIONS

Managers who are efficient communicators are clear, specific, and precise. They use the right words and the right communication channel so they don't waste time.

Inefficient managers say things that result in misunderstandings and communication breakdowns. Inefficient communicators can also take a long time to make their point(s). Everyone knows that person who takes twenty minutes to make a point that could be made in two minutes.

Misunderstanding and communication breakdown occur for a variety of reasons, including:

- Imprecise words
- Missing details
- Verbosity—using more words than needed
- Confusing messages
- Jargon—specialized words and acronyms that some people understand but others don't
- The receiver isn't listening

The best managers avoid these mistakes and always try to communicate in a clear and succinct fashion.

COMMUNICATION PROCESS

The four major parts to the communication process are highlighted in the chart below.

COMMUNICATION PROCESS

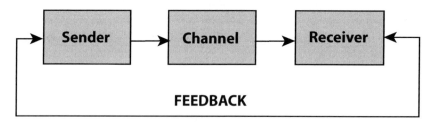

Courtesy of Paul B. Thornton

A. The Sender

The sender, of course, is the speaker. Managers send a variety of messages to a variety of people both inside and outside the company.

Some of the things you can do to be an effective and efficient communicator include:

1. **Know your purpose.** What do you want the receiver to know, think, or do? Why are you communicating this message at this time?

2. **Organize the message.** Keep it simple. Make it easy for the receiver to follow; move from the big picture to progressively more detailed information. Provide the right amount of detail. Too much detail is as bad as too little.

3. **Remove the clutter.** Make your big ideas stand out.

4. **Avoid jargon.** Use words that are precise and understandable.

5. **Provide concrete examples** so the receiver can visualize your point.

6. **Make eye contact** with the receiver. Make sure you have the receiver's undivided attention.

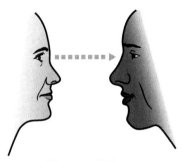

© Kendall Hunt Publishing Company

7. **Consider timing**. There are good and bad times to communicate problems and major changes. You need to determine the best time (and the best way) to convey bad news.

8. **Have a conclusion.** Spell out what you want the receiver to think or do.

B. The Channel

The second part of the communication process is the channel you select to convey your message. Managers can transmit their messages by phone, e-mail, memos, text messages, bulletin boards, one-on-one discussion, group meetings, and "snail" mail. Managers need to select the most efficient and effective channel to deliver their message.

Some of the mistakes made regarding selecting the right channel include:

▶ Scheduling meetings when other channels would be more efficient.

▶ Issuing written warnings and taking other disciplinary actions via e-mail.

▶ Using a channel that your boss doesn't like. Some bosses prefer receiving messages via e-mail; others like face-to-face meetings.

> "First, decide if you need to have a meeting. Many meetings don't need to be held, and often those that are held are attended by more people than necessary."
>
> —Bill Huber former VP Engineering

C. The Receiver

The receiver, of course, is the person listening to the message.

If you ask students what makes a good advisor or employees what makes a good problem solver the answer you often hear is people who listen before prescribing. The best managers are good listeners. They give the speaker their undivided attention.

Here are some things that will help you be a good listener.

1. **Be curious.** Effective listening starts with being motivated and curious about what others are thinking and feeling.

2. **Listen for both the facts and feelings being expressed.** What is the person's energy level? What does their tone of voice indicate?

3. **Eliminate distractions.**

4. **Make eye contact.** This helps you make a connection with the speaker.

5. **Concentrate.** Listening is hard work; your attention can wander. Create a word or phrase you can say to yourself—such as "tune-in" or "concentrate"—as a reminder to listen and stay in the present moment.

6. **Ask questions.** Get the additional information you need to understand the message. Ask the speaker to define terms, provide examples, and add additional details as needed.

7. **Don't shoot the messenger.** Be open to hearing about problems and bad news.

8. **Observe the speaker.** Pay attention to gestures and facial expressions, including smiles, frowns, blinks, and yawns. Look for patterns in how the message is delivered.

After listening to the speaker's key ideas and supporting details, you need to analyze what you have heard. Dissect the information to determine the accuracy, meaning, and significance of the message.

Analysis often includes separating:

▶ The main idea from supporting details

▶ Facts from opinions

▶ What's accurate from what's inaccurate

▶ What's relevant from what's irrelevant

In addition, it is important to determine where the data came from and the sample size that produced the data. Are the speaker's comments based on what three customers said, or on what three hundred customers said? Don't generalize and jump to conclusions that are based on small samples.

D. The Feedback

Feedback is the final step in the communications process. Giving and receiving feedback works as a check to determine if the message was understood as it was intended.

Both the sender and the receiver can solicit feedback.

▶ **Testing the transfer.** After communicating a message, the sender can ask the receiver to explain his understanding of the message. *"Jackson, in your own words, tell me what I want you to do."*

▶ **Paraphrasing or active listening.** First, the listener puts the message into his or her own words. Then, the listener asks the speaker to confirm that s/he has understood the message correctly. *"If I'm hearing you correctly, you asked me to monitor warehouse inventories and give you weekly updates. Is that correct?"*

Jan Morton, President, Self-Us-Team Collaborative

My clients include small business owners as well as managers and leaders from small and large companies. Basically, I'm hired to help an individual or a team be more effective—improve their performance. Improvement means change. The first thing I try to do is determine the level of receptivity. Is the person/team open to change or is there resistance? The client's body language gives me clues as to what's going on which is sometimes different from what they are telling me. There is a difference between "content" and "intent." The words mean one thing, sometimes the inflection or body language tells a different story.

I use a lot of mirroring or paraphrasing of what I'm hearing. I frequently use comments like, "Help me understand your comment about . . ." I often press for specifics. When I paraphrase, I synthesize the content and the intent. I try hard to capture both their words and their deeper meaning. I've also learned it's important to ask questions in a way that doesn't appear I'm looking for a certain answer.

Total focus and concentration on listening is hard work. Being a good listener has helped me understand my clients' real needs and their readiness to change. The big payoff is increased rapport with the client, deeper understanding of what's really going on, and a greater likelihood that what I do will make a positive difference.

SUMMARY

Some things you need to remember . . .

- ▶ The best managers are both effective and efficient communicators.
- ▶ Communication breakdowns can occur during both the sending and receiving parts of the process.
- ▶ Managers need to continuously strive to improve their communication skills.

DISCUSSION QUESTIONS

1. Think about conversations you've had. What is your ratio of asking questions to making comments? What, if any, changes are needed?

2. What is the fine line between communicating too much and too little?

3. Over the past three weeks, you (the manager) have had several opportunities to observe John, a new employee in the production planning department. Your observations include the following:
   - ▶ He is very social and outgoing.
   - ▶ In meetings, John talks a lot and tells long stories. He takes ten minutes to make his point when it should take thirty seconds.
   - ▶ His e-mails and other written messages are usually lengthy and sometimes lack a clear focus.

    a.   Using the directing style of management, what would you say to John?

    b.   Using the discussing style of management, what questions would you ask John?

4. Determine which communication channel (phone, e-mail, text message, memo, one-on-one discussion, or group meeting) you would use in each of the following situations. Briefly explain your decision:

    a.   Issuing a verbal warning

    b.   Informing all employees in your department about a new policy

    c.   Conducting training with employees from Massachusetts, Michigan, and Texas

    d.   Discussing production problems and brainstorming solutions

    e.   Inviting top customers to a "Customer Appreciation Dinner"

    f.   Scheduling a meeting for twelve people

    g.   Determining an employee's home address

    h.   Interview a manager in your community. In a typical day, who does the manager communicate with? What communication channels does s/he use? What types of communication problems has the manager experienced?

GEORGE SMITH CASE STUDY

In your new job as a Manager–Technical Projects, you get an 8:15 a.m. call from a customer requiring an immediate answer. George Smith has been handling the project. You call Smith to your office, but are informed that he has not yet arrived at work.

Harry Lyons, another employee in your group, says he can compile the information, but it will take several hours. You instruct Lyons to call Smith at home. You have an 8:30 a.m. meeting and leave instructions that Smith is to call you as soon as he arrives at work.

At 9:30 a.m. when you return to your office, Harry Lyons tells you Smith still has not arrived. He says he called Smith's home but was unable to get an answer. As a result, he has begun to compile the information on his own. He says it will be ready shortly after noon.

At 10:30 a.m. you get a second call from the customer informing you that a critical situation exists and cannot be resolved until they receive the requested information. The customer is obviously displeased by your inability to respond until shortly after lunch.

At 11:05 a.m. Smith comes into your office. You tell him about the problem with the customer and instruct him to provide you with the information requested as soon as possible.

The customer receives the data at approximately 12:15 p.m. You are informed by the customer that they expect better service in the future.

George Smith is scheduled to meet with you in a few minutes. What will you say to George?

Chapter 15

MAKING PRESENTATIONS

Do your big ideas stand out?

How can you increase the impact of your delivery?

According to mega-bestselling author and business guru Harvey Mackay, the number one skill most lacking in business professionals is public speaking. Today it's challenging to get and hold people's attention. You must be able to present your ideas in a clear, concise, and impactful way.

Managers are called upon to make a number of presentations of varying lengths in a variety of settings. Every presentation you make needs to be effective and efficient.

- ▶ **Effective**—Your presentations need to focus on the right things—address the right issues.
- ▶ **Efficient**—Your presentations should be as long as *necessary* and as short as *possible*. Brevity increases impact.

Here are some things you can do to make your presentation both effective and efficient.

1. **Start with a good introduction**

   a. Connect with the audience in a friendly, authentic, and personal way, just as you would greet a friend. "Good morning and welcome. My name is . . ."

   b. Create interest—give the audience a reason to listen. Address their issues. Solve their problems.

   c. Provide a roadmap of where you plan to take them. "We will discuss three points."

2. **Make your big ideas stand out**

   Just as police officers directing traffic wear orange vests so drivers will notice them, put "orange vests" on your key points so your listeners will pay attention to them. Teach your audience something new. Give them new, fresh insights.

3. **Organize your ideas**

The easiest way to organize your ideas is by creating a list. "Here are five traits of high performing teams." Another proven and easy way to organize your ideas is: problem–solution. That is, you first present a problem, then provide the solution. Keep it simple. Brevity increases impact.

4. **Compare and contrast**

Nancy Duarte, author of the great book *Resonate*, has analyzed many famous speakers and storytellers. She discovered a pattern they all use. They go back and forth between *what is* and *what could be*. Tension builds as they describe what is, then releases as they describe what could be.

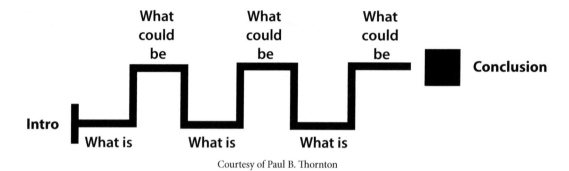

Courtesy of Paul B. Thornton

5. **Support your claims**

Your statements are, in essence, claims. Most people are willing to listen to them, but they need to be convinced before they will accept them and act on them. Back up your statements with facts, statistics, examples, quotations, stories, etc.

6. **Use effective visual aids**

Visual aids are meant to be just that—aids. They should support your presentation, not call attention to themselves. Here are my thoughts regarding slides:

▶ Have one—and only one—major idea per slide.

▶ Use a font size of 32 or larger.

▶ Use pictures and a few words (never more than twelve).

7. **Delivering your message**

One of the most powerful ways you can increase the impact of your delivery is through the use of contrast.

© lightpoet/Shutterstock.com

▶ **Gestures**: Stand perfectly still, then gesture. Increase the effect of your gestures by making them bigger and holding them for several seconds before releasing them.

▶ **Volume**: Alternate your volume. No one likes a monotone voice. Increase your volume or use inflection to emphasize certain points.

▶ **Pause**: Pauses build suspense. They also give listeners a chance to assimilate what you have said and get ready for what you are about to say.

8. **Eye contact**

Mentally divide the room into quarters or thirds, and make eye contact with individuals in all sections. Connect with a person in one part of the room for two to three seconds, then move on and connect with a person in another part of the room.

9. **Regain their attention**

Let's face it—people's attention does wander. You can recapture your audience by using signal phrases that motivate the audience to pay attention: *"This next point is very important." "If you don't remember anything else, remember this . . ."*

10. **Conclusion**

Identify the one thing you want the audience to remember or do.

11. **Practice**

Actors, singers, and athletes all spend hours practicing before every live performance. So should you. Rehearse your presentation until it is polished and you are confident. Dr. Jill Bolte-Taylor rehearsed her highly successful TED talk 200 times before presenting it. Now that's preparation!

SUMMARY

The one thing you need to remember . . .

> ▶ A great presentation requires the 3Ps—preparation, practice, and passion.

DISCUSSION QUESTIONS

1. When trying to support your main points, what is the fine line between providing too much support and not enough support?

2. What is one thing you can do to improve your delivery?

3. Go to the TED Ideas Worth Sharing website (www.ted.com/talks) and observe several speakers. Find a speaker who excels at some aspect of giving presentations. Provide the speaker's name and the one thing you think s/he does very well.

Chapter 16

WRITING MESSAGES

Are your written messages clear and concise?

Managers don't write novels or short stories but they do write:

- ▶ E-mails
- ▶ Memos
- ▶ Reports
- ▶ Supervisory notes
- ▶ Minutes of meetings

Managers must be able to clearly and succinctly express their ideas in writing. Your written messages must be effective and efficient.

- ▶ **Effective written messages** convey the relevant, significant, and important information.
- ▶ **Efficient written messages** are short, to the point, and include the relevant details.

©Imtmphoto/Shutterstock.com

The process of good writing involves three basic steps—preparing, writing, and editing.

A. PREPARING

Think before you begin writing. Some of the questions to think about include:

- ▶ Who is your audience?
- ▶ What is the problem or opportunity they are dealing with?
- ▶ What specifically do you want the reader to know, think, or do?
- ▶ What level of detail is required?

Once you've answered these questions, create a list of the points you want to cover.

B. WRITING

Add details to the list of points you created in the preparing stage. Keep the following in mind as you organize and write your first draft.

1. **Separate key ideas.**

   Each paragraph should have one main point or idea captured in a topic sentence. The topic sentence is normally the first sentence in the paragraph. Each paragraph should be started by an indentation or by skipping a line.

2. **Use bullets or numbers.**

   If you are listing a number of items, use bullets or number your points like I have done in this chapter.

3. **Use short sentences.**

   According to the American Press Institute, sentences with fifteen or fewer words are understood 90 percent of the time. Sentences with eight or fewer words are understood 100 percent of the time. Avoid run-on sentences—two or more complete thoughts are smooshed together. David Ogilvy was often hailed as "The Father of Advertising." He once gave the following advice: "Use short words, short sentences, and short paragraphs." He also said, "Never write more than two pages on any subject."

4. **Make sure you have subject–verb agreement.**

   If the subject of the sentence is singular ("he," "she," or "it"), the verb must also be singular. The pronouns "anyone," "everyone," "no one," and "nobody" are always singular. *She is the leader. Everyone is invited to the meeting.*

   If the subject is plural ("we" or "they"), the verb must also be plural. *We are the new members. They were selected to attend the conference.*

5. **Use proper punctuation.**

   At the end of every sentence there needs to be appropriate punctuation. Use a comma to separate the elements in a series of three or more items: *His favorite colors are red, white, and blue.* Use a comma to set off introductory elements: *After coffee and donuts, the meeting will begin.* Use a comma to separate adjectives: *That tall, distinguished, good-looking professor teaches history.*

6. **Be precise and accurate.**

   Words and phrases like *large, small, as soon as possible, they,* and *teamwork* are vague and imprecise. Be specific. If the manager said, *"I want you to do a good job,"* what does that actually mean? What does a "good job" look like? Without specifics, the employee may interpret your words to mean something different from what was intended. Avoid communication breakdowns by being specific and precise.

7. **Use the correct word.**

   Here are several words that cause confusion:

   ▶ *You're* is a contraction for "you are." *Your* means possession, as in, "your coat."

   ▶ *It's* is a contraction for "it is." *Its* indicates possession, as in, "The dog wagged its tail."

   ▶ *Their* means possession/ownership: "their house." *There* means location. *They're* is a contraction for "they are."

8. **Avoid redundancies and unnecessary words.**

   It is a redundancy to use multiple words that mean or say the same thing.

   ▶ Redundant—*My personal beliefs . . .* Beliefs are personal, so just say, *My beliefs . . .*

   ▶ Redundant—*I decided to paint the machine gray in color.* Gray is a color, so just state, *I decided to paint the machine gray.*

   Avoid unneeded intensifiers or modifiers—words such as *really, very, extremely,* and *severely* are often unnecessary.

C. EDITING

Very few people can sit down and write a perfect letter or e-mail on the first try. The first draft is rarely clear, organized, precise, and grammatically correct. Good writing requires multiple rewrites.

© Rostislav_Sedlacek/Shutterstock.com

Edit your writing by doing the following:

    a.   Read it and concentrate on organization. Are your key ideas organized and easy to follow?

    b.   Read it again and focus on punctuation. Is there a punctuation mark at the end of each sentence? Are commas needed?

    c.   Read it a third time and concentrate on word choice. Are the words clear and understandable? Could some words be replaced with a more precise word?

    d.   Get feedback. Ask someone to read what you have written and see if he or she understands the message you're trying to communicate.

Keep revising your written message until it is both effective and efficient.

SUMMARY

Some things you need to remember . . .

- ► Think before you write.
- ► Make a list of the points you want to cover.
- ► Use bullets or numbers to organize your ideas.
- ► Edit, edit, edit!

DISCUSSION QUESTIONS

1.   Do you communicate more effectively when writing or speaking? Why do you think that is the case?

2.   Correct the mistakes in the following sentences.

    a.   There reporting a significant reduction in inventory.

    b.   The mangers are in they're weekly planning meeting.

    c.   One of the executives are adjusting the sales projections for the 4th quarter.

    d.   Some CEO's only use only the directing style.

    e.   You're a great manager, but and ineffective leader

    f.   A change in accounting procedures can have a big affect on reported earnings.

    g.   After coffee donuts and 5-minutes of socializing the meeting will begin.

    h.   That tall distinguished good-looking professsor teaches history.

    i.   Mary Jean said, the professor that teaches at STCC made several good points.

    j.   He replied "I have no idea what you mean" ?

    k.   After rotting in the cellar for weeks, my brother brought up some oranges.

    l.   We didn't see no results.

    m. I decided to paint the machine gray in color:

3. Rewrite the following job offer so that it includes all the information that the reader needs. (Make up any necessary details.)

    I am pleased to offer you a position at Fontaine and Sons at an annual salary of $35,500. I hope to receive notice of your acceptance soon.

4. You manage John Corcoran. He is the night supervisor of inventory control and shipping. Recently John attended a 9:00 a.m. meeting at corporate headquarters just after working the night shift. Normally, he would have gone home to sleep. Corcoran's work location is about forty-five minutes from the corporate offices.

    Your report of the meeting states: "John Corcoran attended the March 30th meeting on his own time. His input regarding shipping schedule and current inventory issues eliminated the need for guesswork. John's assessment and valuable support permitted the committee to move forward without reservation."

    Prepare an e-mail message you will send John Corcoran to thank him for participating at this meeting. What information do you need to include? Follow the steps outlined in this chapter to ensure your communication is effective and efficient.

Chapter 17

CONDUCTING INTERVIEWS

Do you acquire the right information to help you make the best decisions?

Managers don't just interview job applicants. They also interview customers, suppliers, peers, employees, and consultants. The purpose of conducting an interview is to acquire information.

- ▶ **Effective interviewers** are crystal clear on their goals. They know exactly what information they need to acquire.
- ▶ **Efficient interviewers** have an agenda and they stay on track. They do their homework and thoroughly prepare for the interview.

© Antonio Guiellem/Shutterstock.com

CONDUCTING ANY TYPE OF INTERVIEW

Here are some important points to keep in mind:

1. Determine the information you want to acquire.

2. Prepare questions in advance. Short, simple questions are the most effective.

3. Start with more general questions and then get more specific. Include both open- and closed-ended questions. Open-ended questions can't be answered with a simple "yes" or "no" response. *"Tell me about your findings for the marketing project."* Closed-ended questions can be answered with a "yes" or "no." *"Did you e-mail the client your report?"*

4. Ask one question at a time and then listen. Take notes to capture important information.

5. Ask follow-up questions as needed.

6. Observe body language to gain insights about the full message being conveyed.

INTERVIEWING JOB APPLICANTS

You need to have the right people on your team.

In every organization, job openings occur due to promotions, retirements, and terminations. In addition, as companies grow they need to hire more employees. So, recruiting and hiring are important activities in every organization.

Every manager needs to be proficient at interviewing and selecting the best applicants. To have a great team or run a great operation you need talented and motivated people.

Once qualified candidates are identified, managers typically schedule interviews to select the most qualified applicant. I recommend always interviewing at least five to seven candidates. In addition, it's always useful to interview candidates from both inside and outside the organization. Many companies have job posting systems that allow internal candidates to be the first to apply.

PREPARE FOR THE INTERVIEW

The first thing managers need to do is think about the specific responsibilities and duties of the open position. Some of the appropriate things to do include:

► Review the job description.

► Think about how the job may change in the future.

► Talk to people who currently do the job.

► Think about what it takes to excel in the job.

► Identify the critical knowledge and skills a person needs to excel in this position.

Next, review the applications and resumes of the candidates who have applied.

- ▶ Consider their education, experience, and motivation.
- ▶ Look for the themes in their work history.
- ▶ What have they accomplished?
- ▶ Identify the top candidates for interviews.

It may be useful to start by doing phone interviews to make sure candidates meet the general criteria for the position.

At the end of the interview process, the manager should be able to answer the following questions:

1. Are the applicant's knowledge, skills, and experience excellent, good, average, or poor?
2. Can the applicant excel in all aspects of the job?
3. Does the applicant have the required motivation to do the job?
4. Will the applicant be a good fit on the team?
5. Will the applicant fit the company culture?

CREATE QUESTIONS

The next step is creating questions. The quality of the questions determines the value of the information you get from the applicant. It is helpful to organize questions around themes, such as:

General Information

- ▶ Are you willing to relocate?
- ▶ How much traveling are you willing to do?
- ▶ Are you able to work from 8:00 a.m. to 5:00 p.m.?

Current Job

- ▶ Walk me through what you do on a typical day.
- ▶ What types of decisions do you make in your current job?
- ▶ What is the most difficult part of your job?

Accomplishments

- ▶ How have you improved an important process?
- ▶ What are you most proud of regarding what you have achieved in your current job?
- ▶ In the past twelve months, what's one skill you have improved the most? How did you make the improvement?

Definitions

- ► What is your definition of working too hard?
- ► How do you define teamwork?
- ► How do you define customer satisfaction?

Likes and Dislikes

- ► What did you most like about your last job? Dislike? Why?
- ► What was your favorite course in college?
- ► Tell me about the best boss you have worked for.
- ► Tell me about the worst boss you have worked for.

In addition to the above types of questions, one should ask **hypothetical questions**; that is, provide open-ended scenarios the interviewee must answer.

- ► If you were the team leader, how would you handle . . . ?
- ► If you had a disagreement with a coworker, what would you do?
- ► What steps would you take to plan the summer company picnic for 300 people?
- ► Tell me how you would go about trying to influence your boss to give you a pay raise.

It's important for managers to ask questions that relate to the specific knowledge, skills, and motivation needed to do the job. If the position requires skills in specific areas—such as making presentations, writing, selling, and negotiating—it is very useful to have the applicants demonstrate their skills. For example, having applicants make a ten-minute presentation gives you concrete evidence of how they communicate and organize their ideas. My son, Andy, recently had an interview for a sales position. During the interview the interviewer gave him a pen and said, *"Sell me this pen."* It's helpful to see how each applicant conducts himself in a situation that is close to what he or she will actually be doing on the job.

CONDUCTING THE INTERVIEW

The following is an outline for a forty-five-minute interview:

© Oksana Petrova/Shutterstock.com

- *Introduction/Welcome (2 minutes).* Meet and greet the applicant. Make eye contact, shake hands, and introduce yourself. Make the applicant feel welcome.
- *Icebreaker* (2 minutes). Small talk about the weather, sports, or some other light topic.
- *Getting Information (30 minutes).* Ask questions and listen. Probe, dig, and take notes.

> The major portion of the interview is aimed at getting information from the applicant. My rule of thumb is the 20/80 rule: the manager should do 20 percent of the talking and the applicant should do 80 percent. I once had an interview in which the manager talked 95 percent of the time. He had a big ego and wanted to impress me with all his achievements. But during the interview he learned little about my skills and qualifications.

- *Providing Information (10 minutes).* Give the applicant a realistic job preview. Let the applicant know exactly what the position entails. Describe what it's like to work at your company.
- *Close (1 minute).* Let the applicant know what will happen next. Make sure to provide a specific time frame. *"I will be interviewing three more candidates. I will get back to you within two weeks."*

Immediately after the interview, the manager should review his or her notes and make sure they are complete. Evaluate the applicant's knowledge, skills, and motivation to excel in the job you're filling. Determine each applicant's probability of success and rank the top three candidates.

Invite the top candidates in for a second round of interviews. It can be useful to have several people conduct interviews of the top candidates to get multiple assessments of their talents, motivation, and company fit. Having various people conduct interviews often leads to new insights about potential candidates. Also, it can be useful to interview candidates at different times of the day.

SUMMARY

Some things you need to remember about interviewing . . .

- Start by identifying the information you want to acquire.
- Ask good questions and listen.
- If you recruit and hire great people—listen to their ideas and suggestions.

DISCUSSION QUESTIONS

1. Google "equal employment opportunity" and "affirmative action." In your own words, explain the difference between the two. Do you think Affirmative Action is still important in today's world? Why or why not?"

2. There are a number of laws aimed at protecting employees from discrimination in all aspects of employment. Write a short description of each of the following major laws.
   a. 1964 Civil Rights Act
   b. The Americans with Disabilities Act
   c. The Age Discrimination in Employment Act
   d. The Family and Medical Leave Act
   e. The Fair Labor Standards Act
   f. The Americans with Disabilities Act
   g. The Equal Pay Act
   h. The Pregnancy Discrimination Act
   i. The Occupational Safety and Health Act

3. Interview a manager in a local organization to determine how that organization recruits and selects employees. Come up with a list of at least five questions to ask the manager.

4. Discuss/explain what is wrong with each of the following statements:
   a. I'm not quite sure what we need, but this gal sounds like a super worker.
   b. He's not quite what I'm looking for, but I think he's trainable.
   c. I'm confident this guy can learn a lot from me.
   d. I didn't have time to read his resume, but he had great answers.
   e. This one is such a good fit that I don't need to waste time on a second interview.
   f. After my sales pitch, he was so excited I knew he could do the job.
   g. He's not perfect, but the work is backing up.
   h. He doesn't have a lot of experience, but he seems like a good guy.
   i. Based on the glowing terms I heard from my friend, I'll just skip the reference check.

ROLE-PLAY: CONDUCTING AN INTERVIEW

Assignment: A three-person interview team will be formed to prepare questions to interview applicants for a car sales rep position. The three-person team will conduct a five- to seven-minute interview. Their objective is to gather information through the interview to determine the extent to which the applicant possesses the required job skills.

The key job responsibilities and required skills for the sales rep position are listed below.

- ▶ Selling new and used cars. Meet with customers and ask/answer questions that influence decisions in the car-buying process.
- ▶ Completing all required paperwork to complete a sale.
- ▶ Developing a referral network to help increase the client base.
- ▶ Completing and submitting sales reports and weekly activity reports on a timely basis.

The ideal candidate should have skills in the following areas: communication, listening, influencing, and time management. Sales reps must be able to work some nights and weekends. The three-person interview team will ask questions to evaluate the applicant on the following skills.

1. **Communication Skills**—ability to ask questions and communicate in a clear, concise, and complete way.
2. **Listening Skills**—genuinely interested in understanding what the other person is thinking and feeling.
3. **Influencing Skills**—ability to get the customer to accept your point of view.
4. **Time Management Skills**—ability to set goals, establish priorities, and identify steps to achieve them.

All applicants have had some sales experience at either retail clothing stores or fast-food restaurants. In addition, they will be completing their associate's degree in May. Some candidates played sports in high school and college and participated in extracurricular activities that would illustrate their strengths in each area.

Applicant's Name: _____

Rate the applicant as above average, average, or below average in each of the following skills:

- ▶ Communication
- ▶ Listening
- ▶ Influencing
- ▶ Time Management

Is this applicant a good candidate for the **Sales Representative** position?

YES_____   NO_____

Chapter 18

CONDUCTING MEETINGS

What does it take to run a great meeting?

Meetings are an essential part of virtually every work environment. Every manager is required to plan and run meetings for a variety of reasons, which include:

- ► Establishing goals
- ► Determining roles and responsibilities
- ► Coordinating individual efforts
- ► Obtaining status updates
- ► Collaborating on issues
- ► Brainstorming and solving problems
- ► Garnering support for new proposals

© nd3000/Shutterstock.com

▶ **Effective meetings** have the right topics on the agenda and the right people participating in the discussion.

▶ **Efficient meetings** are productive; they don't waste time.

Meetings that are both effective and efficient can leave you energized and feeling as if decisions are being made and progress is being made.

PLANNING THE MEETING

Good meetings aren't accidents—they are the result of good planning. Planning starts by answering these basic questions:

▶ What is the purpose?

▶ What topics need to be covered?

▶ Who should attend?

▶ When (date and time) should the meeting be conducted?

▶ Location—where should the meeting be held?

The next step is creating an agenda. The agenda lists the topics, desired outcome, time frame, and who is responsible for leading the discussion. An agenda provides a roadmap and helps keep the meeting on track.

MEETING AGENDA

AGENDA ITEM	DESIRED OUTCOME	TIME ALLOTTED	WHO IS RESPONSIBLE

Listing the desired outcomes such as "brainstorm a list" or "make a decision" helps keep the discussion focused and proceeding in the desired direction. Some managers have agenda items but they aren't clear or haven't taken the desired outcome into consideration.

For each agenda item, the manager needs to determine the time frame needed for discussion. The last topic is determining "who is responsible." The manager may delegate the responsibility for leading the discussion on specific items to someone else. It's helpful to send out the agenda in advance of the meeting so people can adequately prepare.

When planning meetings, it's useful to think about the ground rules you want to establish and enforce during the meeting. The purpose of having ground rules is simply to make the meeting more efficient and productive. Typical ground rules include things like:

- Shut off cell phones.
- Listen—one conversation at a time.
- Attack issues and ideas, not people.
- Don't hold back—say what's on your mind.
- Be respectful.
- Start and end the meeting on schedule.

Some managers and team members work together to create a set of rules they agree to follow in every meeting.

Bottom line: Managers need to take time to plan the meeting and prepare an appropriate agenda. Effective meetings require structure and order. It's important to provide adequate time to cover each topic. A common mistake many managers make is they try to cover too much in one meeting.

CONDUCTING THE MEETING

The manager is the leader of the meeting. He or she needs to focus on the agenda and strive to achieve the desired outcomes. Managers leading the meeting typically use all three management styles.

- **Directing**. Some agenda items require the manager to tell the group what must be done by when.
- **Discussing**. There are usually several agenda items that require discussion (that's why the meeting was scheduled).
- **Delegating**. There will be some action items that get delegated to specific individuals.

When the discussion gets off track, it's important for the manager to refocus the group and adhere to the prescribed time schedule.

The manager needs to ask for a volunteer or assign someone to perform the following roles:

- *Timekeeper*—This person needs to monitor the discussion and time schedule and provide feedback to the group as required.
- *Recorder*—This person needs to record the following: decisions made, action items, and open issues. For each action item, the recorder needs to capture the following:
  — What needs to be done
  — Who is responsible
  — When it must be completed

At the end of the meeting, it's helpful to review the action items so everyone is clear on specific assignments and due dates. In addition, after the meeting, it's useful to send out a written summary of the meeting including decisions made and action items.

What should you do when people bring up issues unrelated to the agenda item? Keep a list called the "parking lot." Use a flip chart or whiteboard to capture items that need to be considered for a future meeting.

Managers must deal with a variety of people including some who are unprepared, overly talkative, cynical and negative, and/or have hidden agendas. Make sure each individual has a fair chance of expressing ideas and opinions, but do not let one person dominate the discussion. All participants should be made to feel that their ideas are of equal importance. This may require the meeting leader to directly call on quiet individuals and ask for their opinions or for any ideas they would like to share. This ensures that all ideas and opinions are heard, not just those of the louder or more domineering participants.

EVALUATING THE MEETING

After the meeting, it is useful to do a quick check to see if the meeting was truly productive. Each person attending the meeting evaluates the meeting on factors such as:

- ► How well people listened
- ► Participation level
- ► Decision quality
- ► Leadership
- ► How well the agenda was followed

© ESB Professional/Shutterstock.com

Next, each person provides his or her score. Then there is a discussion from the participants who rated it the highest and lowest. The discussion helps identify what's working and what changes are needed to have more productive meetings.

Managers must demonstrate an openness to feedback and a commitment to improve.

SUMMARY

Some things you need to remember . . .

- ▶ Good meetings don't just happen. They are planned and run by competent managers.
- ▶ The agenda provides the structure and focus for the meeting.
- ▶ The meeting leader must make sure everyone is engaged in the discussion and progress is being made.

DISCUSSION QUESTIONS

1. Think about some of the meetings you have attended. What were some of the factors that made the meeting productive and worthwhile? What were some of the reasons why the meeting was unproductive?

2. You manage a group of thirteen people. You are required to lay off two employees. Create an agenda for the meeting you would have with each employee.

CONDUCTING EFFECTIVE MEETINGS

In-Class Assignment: Conduct a twenty-minute meeting. Submit one piece of paper with the full name of each team member and your responses to the two questions below.

1. Identify the top three behaviors (from the list below) that indicate a team isn't functioning effectively.

2. What can be done to prevent each of the problems you identified?

Assign someone to perform each of the following roles:

- ▶ Leader
- ▶ Recorder
- ▶ Timekeeper

All team members must follow and enforce the following rule: *One person speaks at a time.*

Team Trouble

1. Team members have difficulty following the agenda.
2. Meetings never start or end on time.
3. Broad participation produces minimal accomplishment.
4. The team has split into three subgroups—each having its own agenda.
5. Side conversations are common.
6. Team members air disagreements privately after meetings.
7. Team leader is unwilling to hold people accountable for missed deadlines.

8. Team members hold back their true feelings.

9. The team has great difficulty reaching consensus on any decision.

10. Team members are confused about their roles and assigned action items.

Meeting Process Check

Circle the number that represents your assessment of the meeting you had on "Team Trouble."

(1 = Needs Improvement, 2 = Average, 3 = Good, 4 = Excellent)

Followed Agenda	1	2	3	4
Participation	1	2	3	4
Listening	1	2	3	4
Decision-Making	1	2	3	4
Teamwork	1	2	3	4

Chapter 19

SOLVING PROBLEMS

What are the steps involved in the problem-solving/decision-making process?

In an ideal world, everything runs smoothly. All projects are completed on time and within budget. All processes produce products and services that meet and often exceed customer expectations. But that's not reality. Problems occur—machines break, employees terminate, and errors are made. Every day, managers must deal with a variety of problems and still achieve their goals.

Some problems are routine and easy to solve. Others are very challenging and can significantly impact the business. Fast-paced competition continues to shorten the time that managers have to deal with problems.

- ▶ **Effective managers** take steps to prevent problems from occurring. When problems do arise, they focus on the right ones. Effective managers know to focus on problems that relate to the high priority goals.
- ▶ **Efficient managers** systematically work through the problem-solving/decision-making steps and make timely decisions.

PREVENT PROBLEMS

Some of the actions effective managers take to prevent problems include:

- ▶ **Cross-train employees.** This produces benefits for both the company and the employee. Cross-training gives employees opportunities to learn new skills.
- ▶ **Succession planning.** This is the process of identifying and developing specific people to fill key positions when they open.
- ▶ **Safety policies and procedures.** Establishing safety policies and work rules is critical to preventing accidents and injuries.
- ▶ **Regular maintenance of equipment.** This ensures equipment will consistently perform as needed.

In addition to these actions, effective managers think about what else could go wrong, then take steps to prevent errors and mistakes. Obviously, the more managers can do to prevent problems the better.

EARLY IDENTIFICATION

If you can't prevent a problem, the next best thing is early identification. Control systems are designed to provide timely feedback so managers can take corrective action. There are several types of controls that managers use:

► **Concurrent controls.** Just as your car's dashboard tells you the speed, fuel level, and engine temperature, concurrent controls give managers immediate feedback on performance as it happens. For example, when managers directly observe employees performing an activity they are using a concurrent control system. If an employee is doing something wrong, it can be corrected on the spot.

► Many companies, including retailers like Wal-Mart, Sears, Victoria's Secret, and Home Depot, use point-of-sale cash registers to collect data on each item sold. This is an example of a concurrent control system that immediately updates inventory records so it's clear when replenishment orders need to be placed.

► **Employee feedback.** Effective managers encourage employees to identify problems as early as possible. Early identification of problems provides ample time to take action and get the train back on the tracks.

► **After the fact feedback controls.** This control system provides feedback sometime after something has occurred. For example, managers get budget and production reports that indicate performance for the past month. Managers analyze the data to determine if corrective action is needed in future months.

A manager's level in the organization determines the type of feedback and the frequency of feedback s/he receives. For example, a first-line supervisor may get daily product reports, whereas the director of operations may only focus on weekly production reports.

Too much control is as bad as too little control. Some managers micromanage their employees and put too many controls in place. On the other hand, some managers lack appropriate controls and aren't aware of what's going on or become aware of problems too late to achieve the desired result. The best managers implement the appropriate controls so they get the information they need in a timely fashion.

QUESTIONS TO ASK

When confronted with a problem, managers need to ask themselves the following questions:

1. Is the problem clearly defined?

2. Who owns the problem? (Just because the manager is presented with a problem doesn't necessarily mean it is his to solve.)

3. How much time, effort, and money should go into solving the problem? (Not all problems are equal in importance.)

4. What approach should I use to solve the problem? (Get directly involved, hire a consultant, delegate to an employee, etc.)

THE PROBLEM-SOLVING/DECISION-MAKING PROCESS

There are four steps in the problem-solving/decision-making process:

1. Define the problem
2. Identify possible solutions
3. Evaluate solutions
4. Make a decision

Managers can use any one of the three management styles when dealing with each step in the process.

- ▶ **Directing**. The manager on his own can do each of the four steps listed above.
- ▶ **Discussing**. The manager asks questions and engages his employees in each of the steps.
- ▶ **Delegating**. The manager assigns the problem to one of his employees. The employee then works through each of the four steps.

Managers often use a combination of styles in handling the four steps. For example, the manager may use a directing style for step 1, but then delegate steps 2, 3, and 4 to a member of his staff. In other situations, I have observed managers that use a discussing style for steps 1 and 2 and then delegate steps 3 and 4. However, there are some managers who always use a directing style when it comes to step 4. They insist on making all the decisions. That's not effective. Mature and capable employees need to be empowered and given authority to make certain decisions.

1. Define the Problem

When asked how he would save the world in one hour, Albert Einstein said he would spend fifty-five minutes defining the problem and the last five solving it. Often the hardest part of problem-solving is identifying the real problem. One of my mentors said, *"Beware of people who have a solution before they understand the problem."* The presented issue is often a symptom of an underlying problem. Some managers waste a lot of time putting out fires and never solve the real problem. Like Einstein, managers need to spend time making sure they pinpoint the "route cause" problem. It is always helpful to answer the following questions:

- ▶ **Who?**   Who was involved? Who was not involved?
- ▶ **What?**   What happened? What has changed? What hasn't changed?
- ▶ **When?**   When did it happen? When did it not happen?
- ▶ **Where?**   Where did it happen? Where is it not happening?
- ▶ **How?**   How often does it happen?

A critical component of some quality training programs teaches the "5 Whys Technique." The idea is that if you keep asking "why" you will peel back layers of the onion and eventually identify the real problem. The technique was originally developed by Sakichi Toyoda. It is still used in the Toyota Motor Corporation manufacturing processes.

"Ask Why Five Times/Never Believe the First Report"—signed in the office of Kevin Podmore, Fleet Logistics Manager, Frito Lay North America. Kevin maintains, "The stated problem is often not the real problem. Effective leaders ask lots of 'why questions' to identify the real underlying problem. They also ask 'what if' questions to explore what's possible."

Managers need data in order to define the problem. Data can be divided into two categories: "must have" and "nice to have." Managers will never have the time and resources needed to collect every piece of data, so they need to focus on what's critical. As managers collect data, it's important to separate facts from opinions and what's relevant from what's irrelevant. It's also important to identify who is providing the data. Employees, customers, and senior management may all have very different views of the same problem.

How managers and employees ultimately define the problem is also important. I've heard managers say, *"The problem is we don't have enough computers."* The obvious solution is *"get more computers."* A better problem statement might be *"Work output is 30 percent less than what is required."* That problem statement may lead to a much different discussion of possible solutions.

2. Identify Possible Solutions

Once the problem is clearly defined, one or more options usually come to mind. Force yourself to develop additional solutions. Use brainstorming, benchmarking, and networking to identify additional ways to solve the problem.

- ▶ **Brainstorm**. Get the right group of people together. Try to generate as many ideas as possible. Remove your "judgmental hat" and openly consider unusual, different, and off-the-wall ideas.
- ▶ **Benchmarking**. This is another way to generate new ideas. Research how other companies may have solved the problem.
- ▶ **Network**. Ask people in your network how they have solved this problem or similar problems.

"My first boss told me to never walk into his office with a problem unless I had at least one suggested solution. Now I sing this mantra with everybody I try to help. Thinking about the solution helps you focus on your true vision, not what is getting in your way."

— Beth Goldstein, CEO of Marketing Edge Consulting Group

3. Evaluate Solutions

Managers and employees next need to evaluate each option.

To select the best solution, weigh all the facts and information. Evaluate each option against specific criteria such as cost, warranty, unique features, timeliness, and acceptance by the employees who must do the implementation. Certain criteria may be more important than others. It often makes sense to separate criteria into "must have" criteria and "nice to have" criteria. Other actions managers take to evaluate options include:

- ▶ List the pros and cons.
- ▶ Do a cost/benefit analysis.
- ▶ Consider whether there are resources available to implement the solution.
- ▶ Consider the immediate and long-term impacts. Do you need a short-term fix or a long-term solution? Suzie Welch (wife of Jack Welch and former editor of the *Harvard Business Review* magazine) recommends a 10-10-10-approach. Ask your-self—what impact will this option have in 10 minutes? In 10 months? In 10 years? Will a new precedent be set?

4. Make a Decision

Effective managers and executives are decisive; they make timely decisions.

> "Be willing to make decisions. That's the most important quality in a good leader. Don't fall victim to what I call the ready-aim-aim-aim-aim syndrome. You must be willing to fire."
>
> —Oilman T. Boone Pickens

How should the decision be made? I've heard managers say, *"I'm going with alternative A—the facts support it,"* or, *"Well I like alternative B, call it a hunch."* It's important to consider both the hard data (quantitative data—numbers and facts) and the soft data (qualitative data—intuition and gut feelings) when making a decision.

Even though managers don't have all the data they would like, they must make timely decisions. Some managers suffer from what's called "analysis paralysis." They keep asking for more data, more studies, and more meetings as an excuse so they don't have to make a decision. Managers who can't make decisions become the bottleneck in their departments.

Managers can use any of the following approaches to make decisions.

1. Manager decides (directing style)
2. Group consensus (discussing style)
3. Majority rule (discussing style)
4. Employee decides (delegating style)

Once the decision is made, the next step is implementation. Just making a decision doesn't change anything. Implementation is where the rubber meets the road. Communicate the decisions to all those who have a need to know. Managers must also define who is going to take what actions to implement the decision. Once a decision is made, you need alignment of the troops to do whatever is necessary to take action and make the required changes.

> "When we are debating an issue, loyalty means giving me your honest opinion, whether you think I'll like it or not. Disagreement, at this stage, stimulates me. But once a decision has been made, the debate ends. From that point on, loyalty means executing the decision as if it were your own."
>
> —General Colin Powell

LEARN FROM BAD DECISIONS

We all make bad decisions from time to time. The important thing is to learn from your mistakes. Take some time to reflect on what you missed in your analysis or why the implementation didn't work as expected.

© Constantin Stanciu/Shutterstock.com

SUMMARY

Some things you need to remember . . .

- ▶ Effective managers focus on the right problems at the right time.
- ▶ They use an appropriate management style to engage employees in the problem-solving/decision-making process.
- ▶ Efficient managers use their time productively as they work through each step in the process.

DISCUSSION QUESTIONS

1. What is the fine line between having too many controls and too few controls?

2. You manage a woman who is selling Avon products on company time. This started as a small part of her day, but she is now running quite a business. She keeps a catalog on her desk. Employees return completed order forms and pick up their Avon products at her desk. She has even expanded her reach beyond your group. Up to this point, her work performance was not affected and no other employee has complained. What action, if any, would you take?

3. You receive the following e-mail from your Senior Administrative Assistant, Kelly Reed.

   "I have been with this company for twelve years. My present position with this company is Senior Administrative Assistant. The Wisp-Packaging Company has offered me a position which would give me a 10 percent increase in salary for similar duties. Since I do enjoy my work, I'd hate to leave. However, my financial obligations to my family leave me no choice. My husband recently has been disabled, with no hope of employment for three years. As I mentioned, I have enjoyed my twelve years with this company. I have only taken eleven sick days in the last seven years. My last two performance appraisals were EE—Exceeds Expectations. I need an answer soon."

   The salary range for senior administrative assistants is $33,000–43,000. Kelly's current salary is 41,000 and she received a 4 percent pay increase three months ago.

   Discuss/explain what you would do.

4. Break-even analysis is a technique that is used when evaluating a new product. It computes the quantity of goods a company needs to sell just to cover its costs or break even. A break-even assessment illustrates how difficult or easy it will be to cover costs and make a profit. A product with a break-even quantity that is hard to attain might not be a good product choice to pursue.

   The total cost of producing a product or service is the sum of its fixed and variable costs. A company incurs fixed costs regardless of how much it produces. Fixed costs include overhead, taxes, and insurance. Variable costs are costs that vary directly with the amount of units produced. Variable costs include things like direct materials and labor. Together, fixed and variable costs add up to total cost. Do a break-even analysis of the following:

   Jason Jones, owner of J&J Manufacturing, is considering whether to produce a new product. Jason estimates the fixed costs per year to be $30,000 and variable costs for each unit produced to be $4.00. If Jason sells the product at a price of $7.00, then how many units of product does he have to sell in order to break even?

5. Harris Hotels is considering adding a spa to its current facility in order to improve its list of amenities. Operating the spa would require a fixed cost of $20,000 a year. Variable cost is estimated at $30 per customer. The hotel wants to break even if 10,000 customers use the spa facility. How much should the hotel charge each customer for the spa services in order to break even?

6. Do a Google search on the "balanced scorecard" which was developed by Robert Kaplan and David Norton. What are the benefits of using a "balanced scorecard"?

7. You are the first shift supervisor. You have become aware that one of your employees, Pam Plant, is dating the second shift supervisor, Ryan Pearson. This is a violation of company policy. Today you receive the following phone message from Pearson: "One of your employees, Pam Plant, wants to transfer to the second shift. How about a trade? I'll give you Dee Wright. She's been trying to get in first shift for some time." List all the possible actions you could take.

8. You have been away at a conference for the past five days. Your coworker Dave walks into your office. "Hey," he begins, "it's none of my business but I thought you should know. Last Tuesday and Thursday, I was speaking with Karen Hughes (your employee). She really smelled of alcohol. She really looked washed out." What action will you take?

9. You are Marilyn McClure's manager. She stops by your office and states, "I'm sick and tired of the guys telling dirty jokes, grabbing me, and making references about female anatomy. If it doesn't stop, I'm going to the HR department." What action will you take?

MAINTENANCE MANAGER CASE STUDY

The maintenance department of an automotive plant in Columbus, Ohio, had thirteen maintenance employees. Two of them, Phil Fleming and John Rusin, had great attitudes and were always willing to help coworkers. They were both considered outstanding employees. The quality and quantity of their work were 20–30 percent better than the other maintenance employees' work. Some maintenance workers, and even the maintenance manager, took advantage of them. When the manager made his rounds and found that painting, cleaning, or machine maintenance hadn't been done properly, he would send Phil or John to complete the work or do the job over. Other maintenance employees didn't worry about doing quality work or meeting deadlines. They knew that Phil or John would be sent to bail them out.

The maintenance manager recently complained to his boss, the plant manager, that he was having difficulty coordinating the work of his thirteen employees. The plant manager said, "I have 247 people to worry about. Surely you can handle 13."

In their discussion, the plant manager indicated he was hearing complaints from the production supervisors that several of the maintenance workers were lazy and unmotivated. The plant manager also said that he heard Fleming was looking for a new job.

Questions

1. Define the problem.

2. Imagine you're the maintenance manager. What actions would you take to improve the situation? What style of management would you use? Why?

3. Imagine you're the plant manager. What actions would you take to improve the situation? What style of management would you use? Why?

Chapter 20

RESOLVING CONFLICTS

What are the five approaches managers use to deal with conflicts?

What should managers do when two employees are constantly having conflicts?

In every relationship—husband-wife, manager-employee, leader-follower—there are conflicts. Managers must deal with conflicts that develop between and among employees as well as conflicts they have with customers, bosses, peers, and employees.

- ▶ **Effective managers** focus on the most important conflicts.
- ▶ **Efficient managers** use the most productive approach or method to deal with conflicts.

Is conflict good or bad? Conflict can lead to productive discussions that result in better relationships and improved business operations. Healthy discussion and debate are required to identify the best ideas. Of course, conflicts that lead to yelling and screaming aren't productive. They lead to anger, resentment, lack of cooperation, and hurt relationships.

© HYPESTOCK/Shutterstock.com

QUESTIONS TO ASK

When conflicts occur, there are three questions you need to ask.

1. **Where do we disagree?** I have heard managers and employees say, "*We disagree on everything.*" That's usually not the case. People usually disagree on one or more of the following: goals, plans, priorities, responsibilities, or values. It's important to get specific and figure out exactly where you disagree. For example, "*We agree on the goals but disagree on the steps needed to get there.*"

2. **How important is the issue?** Is it a high, medium, or low priority? Some disagreements should be avoided simply because they are not that significant or important.

3. **How important is the relationship?** I will view a conflict with my wife differently than one with a relative I see every ten years.

APPROACHES TO DEALING WITH CONFLICT

Some of the generally accepted rules of engagement in any conflict include:

▶ Listen to what the other person is saying.

▶ Stay open and be flexible.

▶ Don't bring up past problems.

▶ Avoid threats and accusations.

▶ Be specific and don't generalize.

▶ Focus on finding solutions.

▶ Know when a "cooling off period" is needed.

Psychologists Kenneth Thomas and Ralph Kilmann identified five main styles of dealing with conflict. In 1974, the Thomas-Kilmann Conflict Mode Instrument was introduced. This model maintains that people respond to conflict with different combinations of assertive and cooperative behaviors.

▶ **Assertiveness** is the desire to satisfy one's own needs and goals.

▶ **Cooperativeness** is the desire to satisfy another person's needs and goals.

The diagram below identifies the five approaches:

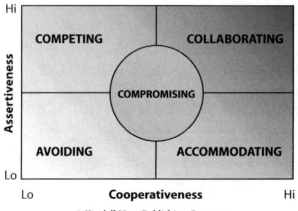

© Kendall Hunt Publishing Company

THE COMPETE APPROACH

When managers use the compete approach—much like participating in sports—the goal is to win. This approach to conflict management produces a win-lose result.

How do managers compete?

▶ They present their case clearly and with authority. They use facts, data, and testimonials to support their position.

▶ They attack the other person's ideas and proposal. They question his assumptions, logic, and create doubts that his approach will really work.

▶ They attack the person. They question the person's credibility, expertise, and commitment.

You often hear politicians using all three of these approaches to beat their opponents.

In what situations should managers use the compete approach? This approach may be appropriate when the conflict involves a manager's core values and beliefs. If the manager has more position power than the other person does, he has the obvious advantage. If both parties have the same amount of position power, it often comes down to personal power. The individual who is more articulate, passionate, and convincing will achieve his goal.

There is a time and place for win-lose competition. However, it's worth noting that the "loser" often goes away angry, plotting his revenge. In some cases, the compete approach produces a lose-lose result. Both parties battle over a long period until each is exhausted and frustrated and neither person achieves his objectives. Effective managers are selective as to when they use the compete approach. They carefully pick their battles.

THE COMPROMISE APPROACH

"Half a loaf is better than nothing."

Compromise is trying to reach a middle ground that is acceptable to both individuals. Compromise produces a win/lose result for both parties. This approach is about negotiations and give-and-take. You get some of what you want but not all.

In what situations should managers use the compromise approach? When managers realize they can't win (get everything they want), the best option may be compromise. *"I bend, you bend."* Compromise can also be a viable option in situations where:

▶ Both parties are open and willing to move from their initial position.

▶ There is a need to maintain a positive relationship with the other person.

Some managers think a compromise must end up close to the middle. For example, if I'm selling my business for $1,000,000 and you offer $900,000, must the compromise price be $950,000? Not necessarily. There are degrees of compromise. I might say my lowest price is $970,000.

People move at different rates from their initial position. In some situations, compromise involves the willingness to try each option for a period of time. *"Let's try your idea for thirty days. Then we'll try my idea for thirty days and compare results."* Compromise is a traditional way to resolve conflicts.

However, effective managers and leaders should never compromise on their values. Cutting corners on your values and core beliefs leads to loss of respect and credibility.

THE COLLABORATION APPROACH

Collaboration involves working together, sharing ideas, and creating new alternatives that benefit both parties. It's based on trust and a willingness to be open and honest. The collaboration approach produces a win-win result—each side gets exactly what they want.

Building trust begins when one party opens up and communicates exactly what he needs and wants. The law of reciprocity says, "Give what you want to receive." If one side opens up, there is a good chance the other side will follow. Collaboration also requires you to be creative and willing to brainstorm, benchmark, and network to come up with innovative solutions. When managers collaborate, they not only produce novel ideas but also build and strengthen relationships with others.

© Rawpixel.com/Shutterstock.com

Effective managers build a culture of openness and trust. They use collaboration as a way to find creative, win-win solutions to their problems and conflicts.

THE AVOIDANCE APPROACH

Avoidance is simply not dealing with the conflict. Managers use the avoidance approach in the following situations:

1. Dealing with the issue will open the proverbial "can of worms."

2. When issues that are more important are pressing.

3. When people need to cool down and regain perspective.

There is a time and place when one should avoid certain conflicts. Not all disagreements need to be worked out. In some situations, it's best to agree to disagree and avoid further discussion.

However, effective managers don't sweep a sensitive conflict under the rug and pretend it doesn't exist. The best managers are willing to have difficult conversations about important topics. Avoiding unpleasant conversations just to keep the peace isn't effective.

THE ACCOMMODATION APPROACH

Give the other person what they want.

Managers use this approach when the issue is more important to others than themselves. In some cases, managers use the accommodation approach to build credits or IOUs for use in the future.

Effective managers know when to accommodate and when to say no to a request. Ineffective managers who overly accommodate employees and customers often set bad precedents that cause future problems.

EVERYBODY IS IN AGREEMENT

It may be groupthink!

A manager wants to discuss a controversial initiative he is proposing. All members of his team nod in agreement and act like they fully support the proposal. In truth, several team members disagree but don't speak up. This is called *groupthink*. Author Alan Webber says that groupthink is nothing more than people not asking questions or making the comments they know they should. In other words—people don't say a word.

Why do some employees hold back their true feelings?

- ▶ Fear of disagreeing with the boss
- ▶ Desire to avoid conflict at all costs
- ▶ Don't want to go against group consensus

What should managers do when they sense groupthink is occurring?

- ▶ Be a "devil's advocate." Disagree with the group. Throw out different opinions and ideas. Strive to get a productive dialog going.
- ▶ Use a structured debate between two conflicting courses of action. Structured debates between plans and counter-plans can be useful before making a decision. One individual might present the case for following "Plan A" and another individual or team argues for "Plan B."

> At Intel, former CEO Andy Grove required his managers to argue and debate issues but once a decision was made they had to support it. His famous axiom "disagree and commit" captures the essence of his philosophy.

© InnerVisionPRO/Shutterstock.com

TWO EMPLOYEES HAVING CONFLICTS

Assume you are the manager and two employees in your group don't get along. They argue, yell and scream, and attack each other on a personal level. Their behavior is affecting the group. What do you do?

1. Meet with each employee individually. Describe your observations. Get their side of the story.

2. Meet with them together. You can use any of the three management styles.

   ▶ **Directing style.** Tell them what you expect going forward. Describe the behaviors that are acceptable and unacceptable.

   ▶ **Discussing style**. Ask questions to get their ideas on what changes are needed and what they are committed to do going forward.

   ▶ **Delegating style.** Tell the two that what is going on is unacceptable. Tell them, "You need to go off and meet on your own. Work out the changes you are committed to make. If you can't work out your difference and establish productive ways to discuss and debate issues, you're both fired. I want to meet with both of you on Monday to hear what decisions you've made."

SUMMARY

Some things you need to remember . . .

   ▶ Conflict is inevitable. Effectively managed conflict is healthy and productive.

   ▶ Each of the five approaches to managing conflict has its time and place.

   ▶ You need to know when and how to use each of the five approaches.

DISCUSSION QUESTIONS

1. In my management and leadership seminars, I often ask participants what advice they have regarding managing conflict effectively. Their comments have included:

   ▶ Build good relationships before conflicts occur.

   ▶ Do not let small issues escalate; deal with them as they arise.

   ▶ Use active listening to show you understand the other person's perspective.

   ▶ Acknowledge feelings before focusing on facts.

   ▶ Show respect for the other person.

   ▶ Be flexible and open. Adapt your style to the situation and people involved.

   What would you add to this list?

2. If one of your employees came to you (the manager) with complaints about another employee, what would you do?

3. Assume you want to go to dinner at restaurant X. Your spouse or friend wants to go to restaurant Y. What are some of the possible ways this conflict can be resolved? Do you think one approach would be better than the others? Explain your reasoning.

4. A manager informs her employee that she is getting a $2,000 merit increase. The employee was expecting a $3,000 increase. Discuss/explain how the manager and employee would behave using each of the five approaches to managing conflict.

5. Interview a manager in a local organization. Determine the kinds of conflicts that occur and the approaches he or she uses to deal with them.

Name _____   Date _____

CONFLICT MANAGEMENT STYLE

Indicate how often you rely on each of the following tactics by circling the number that you feel is most appropriate.

(1= rarely, 3 = sometimes, 5 = always)

1. I argue my case with my coworkers to show the merits of my position.   1   2   3   4   5

2. I negotiate with my coworkers so that a compromise can be reached.   1   2   3   4   5

3. I try to satisfy the expectations of my coworkers.   1   2   3   4   5

4. I try to investigate an issue with my coworkers to find a solution acceptable to both of us.   1   2   3   4   5

5. I am firm in pursuing my side of the issue.   1   2   3   4   5

6. I attempt to avoid being put on the spot and I try to keep my conflict with my coworkers to myself.   1   2   3   4   5

7. I hold onto my solution to a problem.   1   2   3   4   5

8. I use give-and-take to reach a compromise.   1   2   3   4   5

9. I exchange accurate information with my coworkers to jointly solve problems.   1   2   3   4   5

10. I avoid openly discussing my differences with coworkers.   1   2   3   4   5

11. I try to accommodate my coworkers.   1   2   3   4   5

12. I try to bring out all of our concerns so we can arrive at the best possible solution.   1   2   3   4   5

13. I propose a middle ground for breaking ties.   1   2   3   4   5

14. I support the suggestions of my coworkers.   1   2   3   4   5

15. I try to keep my disagreements with my coworkers to myself in order to avoid hard feelings.   1   2   3   4   5

Record your response for each question as noted below. Add your responses together to calculate a total. The style with the highest total is your preferred conflict management style. The next highest total is your back-up conflict management style.

COMPETITION

1. _____

5. _____

7. _____

Total: Competition _____

COLLABORATION

4. _____

9. _____

12. _____

Total: Collaboration _____

AVOIDANCE

6. _____

10. _____

15. _____

Total: Avoidance _____

ACCOMMODATION

3. _____

11. _____

14. _____

Total: Accommodation _____

COMPROMISE

2. _____

8. _____

13. _____

Total: Compromise _____

Primary Style: _____ Back-Up Style: _____

Chapter 21

MOTIVATING OTHERS

What types of things demotivate people?

Performance is a function of a person's knowledge, skills, resources, and motivation. Therefore, the first thing managers need to do is diagnose why the person's performance is below expectations. It may be due to a lack of knowledge or skills, insufficient resources, or lack of motivation. Other factors that may influence performance include having unclear goals, other priorities, and personal or family problems.

> "When I advise a manager about coaching his employee, I suggest that the manager learn what motivates the person. Specifically what does the individual want to achieve? Then the manager must affirm the contributions the person has made and also point out an area to improve. The areas of improvement are related to workplace behaviors; that is, things the employee can do to help self and the team succeed. Effective coaching requires you to ask the right questions and probe when needed. The manager must work for agreement on what specific changes are needed and set a time-frame for improvement. It might be the next day or the next month. Agreement on change and date is essential. Otherwise there will be no impetus for change."
>
> —John Baldoni, President, Baldoni Consulting LLC

MOTIVATING EMPLOYEES

The best managers do a number of things to motivate people.

© Rawpixel.com/Shutterstock.com

1. **Set the example.** If the manager isn't motivated or has a "ho-hum" attitude, his employees will follow his lead. Managers must demonstrate an enthusiastic commitment to their work.

2. **Focus on the mission.** An inspiring mission, such as "end world hunger," motivates people to work long and hard to achieve a notable goal. Remind employees of the larger purpose; the thing they are working toward. The bricklayer who sees his job as building a cathedral to preach the word of God will be more motivated than the bricklayer who only focuses on mixing mortar and laying bricks.

3. **Use the appropriate management style.** Using a management style that fits the needs of employees will motivate them.

   ▶ **Directing style.** Managers motivate employees by assigning goals and deadlines.

   ▶ **Discussing style.** Managers motivate employees by soliciting their ideas and involving them in setting goals and developing plans.

   ▶ **Delegating style.** Managers motivate employees by giving them responsibility and power.

4. **Set goals that are challenging, but attainable.** Employees must believe the goals are attainable. For example, would an incentive of $10,000 for running the 100-yard dash in ten seconds motivate you to get in shape and prepare to run? Probably not! Most people know they will never be able to run the 100-yard dash in ten seconds. The goal is not attainable.

5. **Provide appropriate incentives, rewards, and recognition.** Incentives and rewards must be appealing to the employee and large enough to get his attention.

   ▶ Use appealing rewards and recognition. People's desires and needs vary. For example, my daughter Kate hates to receive public recognition. My wife Mary Jean, on the other hand, loves it. Similarly, for one employee, a trophy is worth all the hard work. For another, a trophy only takes up space and collects dust. As Will Rogers said, "*When you go fishing, you bait the hook not with what you like but with what the fish likes.*"

▶ Use big incentives and rewards. Rewards must be big enough to motivate people to put in the extra effort. For example, in my Principles of Management course I ask students the following question: *"How many of you are willing to do a 10-page book report for <u>one</u> extra point on your next exam?"* No student has ever taken me up on this offer. Why? The reward isn't worth the time and effort. However, when I offer students 20 extra points on the next exam several students become motivated to do the task.

Incentive systems need to be simple and easily understood. Some companies have overly complicated incentive systems that don't motivate their employees.

6. **Provide appropriate negative consequences.** Managers can use "sticks," or punishment, as a way to motivate people. Sticks include anything that is undesirable for the employee such as criticism, verbal and written warnings, required overtime, pay reductions, withholding bonuses, loss of training opportunities, being micro-managed, etc. In theory, the right stick gets people's attention and motivates them to change and improve their performance.

    Like touching a hot stove, the most effective negative consequences are immediate, consistent, and significant. Some managers talk tough, but don't deliver the "stick" or are inconsistent in the way they administer punishment.

7. **Provide helpful coaching, mentoring, and feedback.** Most people are motivated to improve their performance. When managers and mentors provide helpful advice and feedback, it motivates employees to do a better job.

8. **Design jobs so that the tasks are varied, interesting, and meaningful.** Most employees don't want to do the same task over and over. Managers can also use the following actions to make jobs more interesting and challenging.

    ▶ *Job Rotation* involves performing different jobs for a set period of time. For example, employees on a car assembly line could rotate to different operations. The added benefit of job rotation is *cross-training*. Employees learn to perform different jobs so they can fill in for one another when needed.

    ▶ *Job Enlargement* involves adding tasks to broaden job variety. For example, an engineer could be assigned the task of recruiting at several colleges in addition to her project engineering work. At Subway, the roles of order taker, sub maker, and cashier are combined into one, making the job "larger" than the specialized jobs at McDonald's. The idea behind job enlargement is that increasing the range of tasks performed by employees will reduce boredom.

    ▶ *Job Enrichment* is the process of giving employees more power to make decisions and solve problems. *"Owen, I'm giving you the authority to make all decisions on the Systems and Software project."*

How can managers find out what most motivates their employees? Ask them! *"What motivates you?"* Most employees will gladly tell you what they like and dislike. Find out when they are most motivated and least motivated. Managers can use this information to tailor their approach to motivate employees to perform at their best.

DON'T DE-MOTIVATE EMPLOYEES

In some cases, employees show up to work motivated and energized to do their best. Some managers do things that zap their employees' energy and enthusiasm. The following are some things that managers do that de-motivate employees.

▶ **Bad working conditions**—Cramped space, poor ventilation, too hot, too cold, equipment that doesn't work, and dirty work areas can have a negative effect on people's motivation and performance. Managers need to make sure working conditions are comfortable and functional.

▶ **In-groups and out-groups**—Some managers play favorites by engaging, involving, and listening to some employees more than others. This of course de-motivates people in the out-group. Managers need to include equally all members of their group.

▶ **Lack of fairness**—*"John and I worked twenty-six hours of free overtime to complete the project. He received a day off. I received nothing. That's not fair."* Employees want to be treated fairly. The "Equity Theory" of motivation suggests people compare their pay and performance (output) to the pay and performance of some comparison person. The comparison person can be a coworker, a boss, or an average industry pay scale. When people feel they are not being treated fairly, they become de-motivated. People restore equity or fairness by reducing their output or asking for a raise or by looking for a job elsewhere. Bottom line—managers need to make sure they are treating all employees fairly.

Obviously managers must make sure they are not doing anything that de-motivates their employees. They need to provide good working conditions, don't play favorites, and be fair to all employees.

SUMMARY

Some things you need to remember . . .

▶ Create conditions that motivate employees to perform at their best. Make the work environment comfortable, supportive, and professional.

▶ Provide the right carrots and sticks to motivate each person.

▶ Design jobs so that the work is challenging and interesting.

▶ Don't do anything that will de-motivate your employees.

DISCUSSION QUESTIONS

1. What is the fine line between a person being under motivated and over motivated?

2. Do a Google search on the Expectancy Theory model.
    a. Who created the theory?
    b. Discuss/explain the key idea in this theory.

3. Indicate what two things from the list below most motivate you.

    _____ Company mission

    _____ Challenging goals

    _____ Incentive and rewards

    _____ Recognition from others

    _____ Social needs—working in groups and teams

    _____ Achievement—get things accomplished

    _____ Receiving coaching and mentoring

    _____ Doing interesting/creative work

    _____ Money

    _____ Growth and development—learning new things

4. Some theories of motivation are based on the idea that a person's strongest need is what motivates him to take action. Do a Google search on Maslow's Hierarchy of Needs.
    a. Who created this theory?
    b. What needs are included in his hierarchy?
    c. What could a manager do to motivate an employee who has strong safety/security needs?
    d. What could a manager do to motivate an employee who has strong social needs?
    e. What could a manager do to motivate an employee who has strong esteem needs?

5. Discuss/explain David McClelland's Motivational Needs Theory.
    a. What could a manager do to motivate an employee who has a strong need for achievement?
    b. What could a manager do to motivate an employee who has a strong need for power and authority?
    c. What could a manager do to motivate an employee who has a strong need for affiliation?

6. Do a Google search on the Motivation/Hygiene Theory.
    a. Who created this theory?
    b. What is meant by hygiene factors? What impact do they have on a person's motivation?
    c. What are the factors that produce motivated employees?

7. At work, what types of things have your managers done that caused you to be de-motivated?

SALES REPS CASE STUDY

Sales manager Ralph Levine states, "I've got a real problem with my sales reps. They like the action involved in selling but hate to do paperwork. Completing the sales reports and paperwork is frequently put off and then done inadequately. Generally, the longer the delay in writing up a sales report, the more likely it will be incomplete and contain mistakes. This lack of attention to detail hurts when we analyze trends and problem areas. Bottom line—we need clear, detailed, and factual sales reports.

I don't know how to motivate them to write better reports. I have no financial rewards to give them. We're in a budget crunch. In fact, I'll probably have to lay off two sales reps in the next 90 days."

---

1. What would you do to motivate the sales reps to do their paperwork in a timely fashion?

Chapter 22

MANAGING STRESS

What happens when people's demands exceed their coping skills?

If you're a manager, you've probably heard those words from your subordinates and your colleagues. In fact, you've probably thought or spoken them yourself.

And no wonder! In recent years, the pressures of a struggling economy have intensified the already considerable challenges of everyday life. Downsized staffs are causing many managers and employees to work longer hours to accomplish bigger tasks within tighter deadlines. A constant deluge of e-mails and cell-phone calls accelerates the pace and exacerbates the pressures.

Each of us deals differently with the demands we face. The coping skills we employ will vary according to the situation and our own personalities. Some people are more adept than others are at coping with the demands that confront them. But at various times, even those of us with great coping skills are going to feel overwhelmed.

> "Everyone is going to experience stress at some point in their career. I actually think stress is a good thing as it means you are being pushed beyond your limits, so in essence you have the option to do something positive with it and grow. The key though is to figure out how to manage through that stress without causing discord with your team or harming yourself. Walk away, grab a workout, talk to a confidant—just don't hold it in and 'hope' it is just going to go away because it won't."
>
> —Kate Labor, Vice President-Support Services, Systems & Support

When the demands we face exceed our capacity to cope, we will suffer a stress reaction. This dynamic can be expressed as follows:

$$D > CS = SR \text{ (Demands > Coping Skills = Stress Reaction)}$$

Stress impacts the effectiveness and productivity of both managers and employees. When stress reactions are minimized, people are more physically, mentally, and emotionally refreshed. They work harder and enjoy their work more. Their efforts are more productive, their careers are more successful, and their lives are more fulfilling.

DEMANDS

Demands vary in type and prevalence from day to day and from individual to individual. Demands in the workplace include the following:

- ▶ Downsizings and high turnover
- ▶ Radically increased workloads
- ▶ Tight deadlines
- ▶ Interpersonal conflicts
- ▶ Difficult coworkers and customers
- ▶ Changing priorities and unclear goals
- ▶ Excessive travel
- ▶ Micromanagement
- ▶ Relocations
- ▶ Worry about layoffs
- ▶ Hurt feelings or anger due to the actions or inactions of others

© AVAVA/Shutterstock.com

Demands outside of work, which may come from family and/or friends, can include the following:

- ► Interpersonal conflicts
- ► Parenting responsibilities
- ► Caregiving responsibilities for elderly parents or young children
- ► Extra effort, expectations, and memories associated with holidays and special occasions
- ► Time required for household chores
- ► Struggle to spend quality time with spouse, children, and/or friends

Reducing Demands

As a manager, you should be aware of the demands that confront you and those who report to you. Periodically step back and ask yourself questions such as the following:

- ► **What can I stop doing?** What meetings, paperwork, and record keeping can I eliminate? What reports do I write that no one reads?
- ► **What can I do less of?** How can I reduce the time I spend in meetings? Can I reduce the number of e-mails I receive? How can I decrease the interruptions from phone calls?
- ► **What can I delegate?** Am I holding on to some tasks simply because I enjoy doing them, or perhaps because I don't trust others to do them adequately?
- ► **What can I do differently?** Can I streamline some procedures? Should I increase my staff's involvement in goal setting and planning?

COPING SKILLS

Everyone employs coping skills to deal with demands. Unfortunately, the skills and strategies some people use are counterproductive, even destructive. Excessive drinking, smoking, taking drugs, denying reality, playing victim, and blaming others may provide temporary escape from stressful demands. However, these types of coping mechanisms create new and bigger problems over the long run.

Managers should constantly strive to strengthen their personal coping skills and the skills of those reporting to them. Here are some helpful suggestions organized by four major categories:

- ► **Time Management.** Improve your ability to set goals, prioritize tasks, and reduce distractions. Learn to say "no" to some requests.
- ► **Emotional Intelligence.** Become aware of your feelings so you can channel them in positive directions.
- ► **Exercise.** Join a health club; hire a personal trainer; walk or jog daily; ride a bike; swim; play an organized sport; take breaks during the day to walk or get fresh air; maintain a healthy balance between work and play.
- ► **Relaxation.** Take yoga classes; treat yourself to a massage; practice meditation and deep breathing; watch high-quality TV programs, especially ones that make you feel good or laugh; listen to music; jump in a hot tub; take regular vacations and mini-vacations.

There are many good sources that managers and employees can use to improve their coping skills, including seminars and workshops, books and magazines, YouTube videos, and advice from mentors and coaches.

Gary Lockwood, Founder, CEOSuccess.com, states, "I try to reduce demands and fully utilize my coping skills. I frequently review my demands to see which ones I can 'let go' of. Letting go means I say 'no', delegate, or outsource. This is the time I need to be brutally honest and decide what requires my attention. I can't do everything, so I choose those demands that have the biggest impact on my business or have the strongest influence on my happiness and well-being.

As for coping skills, exercise is the fastest way for me to dissipate stress. Taking a long walk with my wife will drop my stress immediately as we talk about the future, our grandchildren, upcoming vacations, and so on. My second coping action is to schedule days off, relaxation time, every 4-6 weeks. These mini-vacations help me recuperate both physically and emotionally."

STRESS REACTIONS

© Oliyy/Shutterstock.com

When the demands confronting an individual exceed the individual's ability to cope, a stress reaction occurs. Stress reactions undermine performance, disrupt relationships, and impair health. The formula—**D > CS = SR**—is a useful tool for minimizing stress reactions. It reminds us that stress should be combated both by reducing demands and by increasing coping skills.

Stress impacts the effectiveness and productivity of both managers and employees. High levels of stress can be debilitating. Excessive stress can lead to:

▶ **Behavioral reactions** like yelling, screaming, backbiting, and even fighting.

▶ **Physical reactions** such as headaches, ulcers, stomach distress, muscle tension, problems with sexual performance, and sleeping.

▶ **Psychological reactions** including anxiety, anger, mood swings, and difficulty concentrating.

SUMMARY

Some things you need to remember . . .

▶ Take steps to minimize the demands you and your employees face.

▶ Constantly seek ways to improve your coping skills and the coping skills of your employees.

DISCUSSION QUESTIONS

1. What can you do to reduce your demands?

2. What can you do to improve your coping skills?

JIM O'BRIEN: SALES REPRESENTATIVE CASE STUDY

Jim O'Brien impatiently drummed the steering wheel and puffed a cigarette. His car moved slowly, northbound along Route 128 toward Boston. Heavy traffic was normal in the mid-afternoon. In any event, it was another irritation that was going to make him late for his next appointment.

He was a sales representative for Manco School Supply Company, which sold school supplies to schools and colleges. His sales were down due to increased competition. Other school supply companies were eager to grab new accounts so they were offering discounted prices and special incentives. It was becoming more common for schools to switch from one supplier to another to save a buck. Jim pressed his half-finished cigarette against the ashtray and accelerated the car into another lane.

The buyers in the school systems knew that the market was in their favor. Many were demanding price discounts and faster delivery times. Earlier in the week, one of Jim's more demanding customers telephoned for another shipment of paper and notebooks to be delivered the next morning. To meet this deadline, Jim had to complete an "expedited delivery form" and then personally convince the shipping group to make the delivery by 10:00 a.m. Jim disliked making expedited delivery requests because it took extra time and annoyed the shipping department. Discounts were even more troublesome because they reduced his commission and were frowned upon by Manco's management.

Jim's boss, Jack Sweeney, was putting pressure on all the sales reps to increase sales by 20 percent. Sweeney complained the reps weren't aggressive enough to open new accounts and close on sales. Jim reached for his large Dunkin Donuts coffee.

Two months earlier, Sweeney had a "little chat" (as he called it) with Jim about the stagnant sales in his area and the recent loss of a major account to the competition. Jim became nervous about his work and began having sleepless nights. To increase sales, Jim began making more calls to new clients, even in remote areas of Maine and New Hampshire. Most nights he arrived home after 7:00 p.m. and then had to do his paperwork. The long days put a strain on his relationship with his wife and two children, ages ten and fourteen.

To make matters worse, Manco was considering acquiring another school supply company. Rumors of layoffs were frequent. Jim felt his job was in jeopardy. Jim felt another headache coming on as he stared at the endless line of red taillights.

Currently, there was an "Event Planner" position open in the marketing department. Although Jim had the basic qualifications for this position, he liked being out on the road. He hated the idea of sitting behind a desk all day. However, his wife liked the idea because it would involve less travel and a steady salary. His current salary included a base of $2,000 per month plus commission, which fluctuated between $1,000 and $4,000 per month.

The loud honk of another car startled Jim as he swerved into the exit lane that he was supposed to take (but almost missed). A few minutes later, he pulled into Revere High School's parking lot. Jim hadn't eaten since 8:00 a.m., but had managed to down his usual four cups of coffee. He rummaged through his briefcase for some aspirin to relieve the headache. Jim sighed as he glanced at his watch—only thirty-eight minutes late for the appointment.

Assignment

1. Create three questions you will ask your classmates to discuss the significant points in this case study.

Chapter 23

DEALING WITH DIFFICULT PEOPLE

What are some of the best ways to deal with difficult people?

Managers deal with a wide range of personalities. Most people are cooperative and reasonable. However, some employees—including bosses, peers, and employees—can be very difficult to deal with. As one human resources manager said, "Difficult people are totally focused on their own agendas and needs. They cause tension and conflicts. Difficult people are tedious and time-consuming."

- ▶ **Effective managers** stay focused and hold people accountable for completing tasks on time and maintaining a positive relationship with coworkers.
- ▶ **Efficient managers** don't waste their time and energy getting sucked into the high drama some difficult people can cause.

GENERAL POINTS

Some of the types of difficult people managers must deal with include:

- ▶ The aggressor
- ▶ The victim
- ▶ The rescuer
- ▶ The perfectionist
- ▶ The procrastinator

Some general points to keep in mind when dealing with any type of difficult person include:

1. Don't just ignore the difficult person, manage around him or her, or hope the employee quits.

2. Preparation is important. Steven P. Cohen, President of The Negotiation Skills Company, Inc. and author of *Negotiating Skills for Managers*, writes, "Self-knowledge and good preparation are critical tools for dealing with annoying people." Be clear on your goals. Have a plan on how you will proceed.

3. Effective communication is always important but never more so than when dealing with a difficult person. Listen carefully and make sure you understand the person's point before you respond. Michael Beck, author of *The Insurance Coach,* says, "Take the time to understand the other person's motivation for acting the way they do. If you're effective at this, you'll be able to either help them change their perspective on things or help them to move on to something that better suits them. This solution is about helping people grow and maximize their talents."

4. Don't use defensive-provoking statements. Comments like, "You're an idiot" will surely put the other person on the defensive. It is also important for managers not to react defensively. Stay calm and open.

5. Try to understand the other person's goals and objectives. What's their agenda? What do they want or need?

6. Explain your expectations. Tell or ask the person to identify one or more actions they need to take to improve.

7. Schedule follow-up meetings. Let them know where they have improved and what areas still need improvement.

THE AGGRESSOR

"I hate dealing with Warren. He's such a bully."

Aggressive people assert personal dominance to get their way. They are strong-willed and have an *"I'm right, you're wrong"* attitude. They see no weaknesses in themselves and constantly find flaws in others. Aggressive people react with hostility toward anyone who is blocking progress. They talk over people and refuse to listen. Their favorite approach to managing conflicts is "compete" and, of course, they must win. They are very task-oriented and don't spend time building effective relationships with their colleagues.

Some of the words and phrases used to describe aggressive people include:

► Sherman tank
► Demanding
► Domineering
► Bull in a china shop
► Know-it-alls
► Sarcastic

Why are aggressive people tolerated? They generally work hard and get things done. The problem is, they leave a lot of upset and demoralized people in their wake. Sometimes it's not what they say but how they say it. Their condescending tone is annoying and upsetting to coworkers.

Tips for dealing with aggressive people:

► **Remain calm**. Take a deep breath.
► **Match their position**. If they are standing, then you stand. If they are seated, then you sit, too.

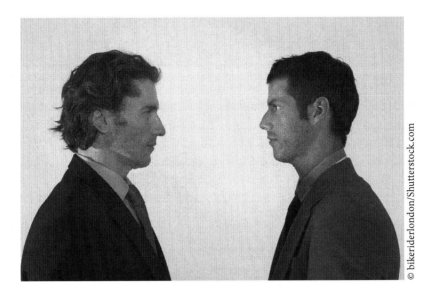

- ▸ **Name the behavior**. *"You're yelling. Do you mean to?"*
- ▸ **Establish ground rules**. *No yelling. No interruptions when speaking. I'll listen to you, but then you have to listen to me.*
- ▸ **Paraphrase what they are saying**. Aggressive people aren't used to people really listening to them.
- ▸ **Coach them** on the importance of not only getting the task done, but also building positive relationships with coworkers. Building relationships requires them to be open, listen, and fully consider other people's ideas.

THE VICTIM

"Emma likes to complain and blame everyone for her problems."

Victims like to talk about all the things going wrong in their lives. Harvard researchers Robert Kegan and Lisa Laskow Lahey describe victims as "BMW" people. No, they don't drive BMWs, but rather they bitch, moan, and whine. They are quick to blame others, even when it is clearly their fault for not getting the task done. They also tend to be very negative people. They are the first to point out why an idea won't work.

Eileen Odum, President, National Operations, Verizon, New York City, picks up on the whine factor. She states,

"Few behaviors are more annoying to me than adults who whine—especially in the workplace. I had a new recruit who thought I would enjoy hearing about everything from his troubles with his landlord to how difficult his performance objectives were to achieve. He must have thought that was part of our growing relationship. Maybe he had a mother or sister who gave him a lot of sympathies for that behavior, but I'm not a person who commiserates in that way. That's every day, get-over-it stuff and whining to me about it shows a lack of sensitivity and maturity."

Leaders don't whine and complain. They don't play the victim role. Rather they face reality and deal with what is in front of them.

"No Whining"

—Sign on the desk of James Parker, former CEO, Southwest Airlines.

Some of the comments I've heard victims make include:

- ▶ "I have little to no power at the office."
- ▶ "Why does this always happen to me?"
- ▶ "There is no hope for relief. It will never change."
- ▶ "They won't give me the information I need."
- ▶ "I always get the worst projects."

Victims often come across as helpless. Their attitude is "People don't understand how bad I have it." A student in one of my courses said, "*Victims are depressing to be around. They feel sorry for themselves and don't take any responsibility for making changes.*"

Tips for dealing with victims:

- ▶ **Focus on the present and future**. Victims like to rehash things that happened in the past.
- ▶ **Ask the victim to prioritize his problems**. Only address the key issues. Don't get tangled up or bogged down in the minutia. Dig for specifics. Victims like to make broad, sweeping generalizations.
- ▶ **Keep ownership of the problem with them**. Facilitate a discussion to help them choose an appropriate action to address their top problem. Quality consultant William H. Denney, Ph.D. says, "*Talking about complaints without solutions is unproductive and time-wasting.*" Identify the next steps the person will take.
- ▶ **Coach them** on the importance of being responsible.

THE RESCUER

The rescuer is the person who's always willing to help others. They are people pleasers. Their major need is to be liked and appreciated. "I'll help" are their favorite words. Rescuers like to jump in and save the day. A consultant remarks, "*The rescuer avoids confrontation. They're 'yes' people. They say 'yes' without thinking through the implications. They over-commit to others and don't get their own work done.*"

Early on, managers are often impressed with the rescuer's willingness to help. "*Gene is a real team player. He's the first person to volunteer to help.*" But, managers soon find out that rescuers don't get their core job tasks completed.

Some of the comments I've heard rescuers make are:

- ▶ "It was my responsibility to take care of people."
- ▶ "I have a strong motivation to help others, even if it means I have to stay late."
- ▶ "I habitually tried to solve other people's problems."
- ▶ "I know this is your project, but let me add it to my list to take the burden off of you."

Tips for dealing with rescuers:

- ▶ **Monitor closely**. Keep a list of all the committees and task forces they are on.
- ▶ **Remind them** of their core job responsibilities.
- ▶ **Coach them** on the importance of doing their core job and the dangers of over-committing.

© Happy Stock Photo/Shutterstock.com

THE PERFECTIONIST

"She expects everything to be perfect!"

Candace Moody, VP, Communications for a non-profit organization pointed out, *"You've all seen her— she's the harried middle manager who stays in the office until 10 p.m., editing and re-editing a report that her boss will only glance through. He's the guy whose projects die on the vine because he can't finalize a plan or finish the funding request."*

Perfectionists operate on the assumption that there is one perfect answer. A finished product that is "good enough" would never satisfy a perfectionist.

The big problem with perfectionists is that they try to be perfect at everything. The perfectionist pushes himself—and others—too hard and too long. In today's fast-paced and demanding world, it's impossible to be perfect at everything. The perfectionist needs to realize that it's okay to do just "good" or "average" on some tasks.

Some of the things I've heard people say about perfectionists include:

- ▶ "He's never satisfied."
- ▶ "She's arrogant. She doesn't think anyone can do the task as well as she can."
- ▶ "Unrealistic standards on things that don't matter."
- ▶ "Revision after revision after revision."
- ▶ "Why bother—you know it's never going to be good enough."

Tips for dealing with perfectionists:

- ▶ **Emphasize deadlines and get their commitment.**
- ▶ **Monitor their work.**
- ▶ **Coach them** on the importance of the 80/20 rule. Eighty percent of the tasks don't require perfection. Meeting deadlines needs to be a top priority.

THE PROCRASTINATOR

"I'll do it next week. I've got plenty of time."

The procrastinator leaves tasks and assignments to the last minute. They throw themselves and others into a panic to meet the deadline. Rita Emmett, professional speaker and author of *The Procrastinator's Handbook,* says that when procrastinators have a big project, they often become overwhelmed. They don't know where to start.

Some of the typical things procrastinators say are:

▶ *"There isn't enough time in the day for everything I have to do!"* This is often said because they have mismanaged their time doing something other than their most important task.

▶ *"I've got it under control"*—a typical response when you ask if the project will be completed on time.

▶ *"I'm waiting on some additional information before I get started."* (Although the information needed is something that can be inserted later.)

Tips for dealing with the procrastinator:

▶ **Break tasks down** into bite-size pieces.

▶ **Establish deadlines** to begin and end tasks.

▶ **Monitor closely**.

▶ **Coach them** on the importance of meeting deadlines.

SUMMARY

Some things you need to remember . . .

▶ "Difficult people" often have blind spots and aren't fully aware of what they are doing or how they come across to others.

▶ Coach them, so they become more aware of their behavior and the consequences of their behavior.

▶ Identify one or two actions they can take to improve their performance.

▶ Reward and recognize them when you see improvements.

DISCUSSION QUESTIONS

1. What other types of annoying behaviors or difficult people have you encountered?

2. What techniques or approaches do you use to deal with difficult people?

THE RESCUER CASE STUDY

As a senior project manager at a public utility company, Mitchell had thrived in the company for nearly twelve years. His team of twenty-four engineers was effective and efficient in doing their jobs. They were a cohesive team. They were often the source of creative ideas that helped other departments. All that changed, however, when the utility's board brought in a hard-charging CEO and made Mitchell one of his direct reports. Mitchell states, "The CEO walked all over people. He made fun of them, intimidated them, and criticized work for no reason. One of our project managers was hospitalized with ulcers. One executive took early retirement. People throughout the organization were running scared. Eventually, they spent most of their time complaining and sending out resumes. However, under the new CEO, sales increased slightly in his first year and expenses were cut 3 percent the first year and 6 percent the second year."

Rather than watch the organization come to a standstill, Mitchell stepped between the new CEO and his colleagues. He allowed people to vent their frustrations to him behind closed doors. At meetings, when the CEO picked on coworkers, Mitchell stood up for them, often taking verbal beatings for his intervention. On occasion, he played the role of front man for the CEO. He translated the CEO's "killer goals" and seemingly irrational directives so that people could put them into action. He even defended the CEO: "He's not such a bad guy. He wants the best for the company."

Mitchell kept at it for almost two years, until the board fired the CEO. By then, however, Mitchell was considering leaving, not just the company, but also his profession. "I was exhausted, burned out," he says. "In the end, I stayed with the company, but I took a year off from being a manager and just worked with the team. I had to recharge."

Assignment

Create three questions you will ask your classmates to discuss the significant points in this case study.

Chapter 24

MANAGING YOUR CAREER

Who is responsible for your career?

What can you do to achieve your career goals?

There are four important steps involved in managing your career:

1. Increase self-awareness.

2. Take action.

3. Sell yourself.

4. Develop yourself.

INCREASE SELF-AWARENESS

The more you know about yourself, the better. The most effective managers and leaders know who they are and what they stand for. Write down your answers to the questions below as a first step to increase your self-awareness.

- ▶ **Define your mission, vision, and values.** What's your purpose? What's your long-term vision of your career and personal goals? What are your values and guiding principles?

- ▶ **Do a personal SWOT analysis.** What are your strengths, weaknesses, opportunities, and threats?

- ▶ **What's your competitive advantage?** What is your greatest strength? What do you do better than your peers?

- ▶ **What's your passion?** What gets you excited? What do your hobbies indicate you most like to do? What issue makes you most upset or angry? What problem would you like to solve? If you were invited to give a speech on any topic, what topic would you choose? Why that topic?

Remember what Steve Jobs said, *"I'm convinced that the only thing that kept me going was that I loved what I did. You've got to find what you love. And that is as true for your work as it is for your lovers. Your work is going to fill a large part of your life, and the only way to be truly satisfied is to do what you believe is great work. And the only way to do great work is to love what you do. If you haven't found it yet, keep looking. Don't settle. As with all matters of the heart, you'll know when you find it. Your time is limited; don't waste it living someone else's life."*

▶ **Take the Myers-Briggs assessment.** What does your personality profile say about you? What type of career fields best align with your interests and personality?

▶ **Define success.** How do you define "success"?

It takes time, effort, and reflection to answer these questions. It's actually a lifelong journey. It will require multiple iterations before you will be satisfied with your answers. In addition, your answers will change over time. So keep at it until you fully understand who you are and what you believe.

TAKE ACTION

There are a number of things you can do to succeed in your current job and prepare yourself for future advancement.

▶ **Identify the next two jobs you want.** It's difficult to say what you will be doing ten years from now. Your career path will not be a straight line. It will zig and zag. Heather Mundell, life and career coach, says that the most valuable advice she received about career management was to always be thinking a couple of steps ahead. You can get lost in the minutiae of your daily tasks and lose sight of a bigger picture. It's important to take time to think about the next one or two positions you want to pursue.

▶ **Deliver results in your current job.** Separate yourself from the crowd by doing great work. Take on difficult and visible assignments. You will not be given more responsibility and a bigger role if you're an average performer in your current job.

▶ **Conduct information interviews.** Ask people about their jobs—especially those jobs you may want to pursue. How do they spend a typical day? What types of decisions do they make? Whom do they interact with? What do they most like and dislike about their jobs?

▶ **Grow your network.** Networking is a systematic approach to making contacts and building professional relationships. Your network can help in many ways, including:

— Providing information on specific job openings and skill requirements

— Giving advice and guidance on work problems

— Pointing out best practices

— Identifying job opportunities

— Recommending articles, books, and seminars to attend

Start building your network with your family, friends, and colleagues. Get plugged into what's happening in your profession and industry. Join professional associations. Attend conferences and seminars. Use Web-enabled technologies such as LinkedIn and Facebook to build your network. Subscribe to industry publications. Keep a list of the people you meet. Remember—networking is a two-way street. You must give to get. Always be on the lookout for useful information and helpful ideas you can pass along to people in your network.

▶ **Utilize mentors.** All managers and employees can benefit from having a good mentor. Mentors provide advice and guidance you won't find in a book. With a mentor, you form a close, personal relationship. Generally, a mentor is an experienced person you admire, someone who has accomplished what you want to achieve. Mentors help develop a protégé's abilities through advising, coaching, tutoring, providing emotional support, and being a role model. Your mentor is an objective outside resource that can give you a fresh perspective.

© Monkey Business Images/Shutterstock.com

"A mentor is someone who sees more talent and ability within you, than you see in yourself, and helps bring it out of you."

—Bob Proctor

▶ **Help your boss achieve success.** When your boss gets promoted or leaves for a big job, guess who he is going to want to take along with him? Every boss wants employees who are committed to helping him/her succeed.

SELL YOURSELF

Every successful sales rep will tell you that the first step in selling anything is to understand the needs, problems, and goals of the buyer. You need to understand the needs of the hiring manager.

▶ **Update your résumé.** Your résumé is the first thing potential employers see. It's critical to have a résumé that is professional and sells your talents and skills. Your résumé should include your core job responsibilities and your key accomplishments. Indicate what you have done to make a difference in the jobs you've held. For example, how did you increase sales, cut costs, improve quality, or increase customer satisfaction?

▶ **Perfect your elevator speech.** In one minute or less, can you clearly and succinctly explain your key strengths, accomplishments, and how you can help the hiring manager? You may be a star, but can you sell yourself in a convincing way?

▶ **Keep a running list of your accomplishments and skills**. Maintain a portfolio that includes examples of your best work.

DEVELOP YOURSELF

In an ever-changing world, you need to keep your knowledge and skills up-to-date. Here are a few things you can do:

▶ **Periodically check job ads.** What skills and certifications are companies looking for? What new attitudes and expectations do employers have of their employees?

▶ **Practice continuous learning.** Spend 80 percent of your time building your strengths and 20 percent correcting your weaknesses. Below are some suggestions and resources that can help you.

— *Internet*—There are many great websites offering good articles, videos, and slides that relate to business, management, and leadership. Some of my favorites include leader-values.com, great-leadershipbydan.com, smartleadership.com, and tompeters.com. YouTube.com provides video instruction on a full range of management and leadership topics. Slideshare.net provides the slides people have used to discuss a wide range of business topics.

— *Seminars and Workshops*—There are many good seminars that focus on all aspects of management. Check out the following: American Management Association, Center for Creative Leadership, and The Cape Cod Institute.

— *Books and Magazines*—There are many excellent business books and magazines that provide up-to-date articles and advice on management and leadership. Some of my favorites include *Fortune*, *Fast Company*, *Harvard Business Review*, *Success*, and the *Leader to Leader Journal*.

— *Podcasts, MP3's, and Audiotapes*—No time to read? Audio-Tech Business Book Summaries and Soundview Executive Book Summaries provide excellent audiotapes on a wide range of business topics. In addition, there are many great podcasts offered online.

— *Coach*—Volunteer to coach an athletic team. This is a great way to work on your skills by communicating, establishing goals, making decisions, and motivating players.

▶ **Solicit feedback.** Periodically ask your bosses, customers, peers, and direct reports for feedback. Be open and consider what people have to say about your strengths and areas needing improvement.

▶ **Develop your emotional intelligence.** Your ability to understand your emotions and channel them in a positive direction is an important ingredient of success. Equally important is your ability to have empathy and understand how others are thinking and feeling.

▶ **Drop your anger.** No one likes an angry, bitter, resentful person. The business world isn't always fair. You may not always get the promotion you deserve. You may not always get the pay raise you earned. You may not get selected for the high potential program. If you stay angry and bitter, you stop growing and developing. See what you can learn from the experience and then move on.

SUMMARY

Some things you need to remember . . .

▶ You own your career.

▶ Achieving your career goals requires reflection, planning, and action.

▶ Use your network and mentors to help you achieve your career goals.

DISCUSSION QUESTIONS

1. You have just been hired as a management trainee for a manufacturing company—it's your first day! You are scheduled to meet with your boss that afternoon. She said that you should send her an e-mail with some of your questions so that she can be better prepared for the meeting.

   What are the top three questions that you will want to discuss?

2. Identify your strengths. From the list below, select your three strongest skills. Feel free to add any additional skills.

   ▶ Asking Questions
   ▶ Building Relationships
   ▶ Coaching
   ▶ Communicating
   ▶ Creating and Innovating
   ▶ Delegating
   ▶ Directing Others
   ▶ Establishing Goals
   ▶ Establishing Priorities
   ▶ Inspiring Others
   ▶ Interviewing
   ▶ Leading
   ▶ Learning
   ▶ Listening
   ▶ Making Presentations
   ▶ Managing Stress
   ▶ Managing Time
   ▶ Motivating Others
   ▶ Negotiating
   ▶ Networking
   ▶ Planning and Organizing
   ▶ Providing Feedback
   ▶ Resolving Conflicts
   ▶ Solving Problems
   ▶ Writing
   ▶ Other:_____
   ▶ Other:_____
   ▶ Other:_____

ERIC'S CAREER MANAGEMENT—CASE STUDY

Eric graduated from Springfield College with a bachelor's degree in sports management. During college, he played varsity basketball and baseball. His summer jobs included youth camp counselor and working at an ice cream shop. After receiving his bachelor's degree, he entered a master's degree program in sports management. During the next two years, he did an internship with ESPN and was an assistant coach for both the basketball and golf teams. When asked what he wanted to do after completing his master's degree, he said, "I'd like to get a job in sports administration, maybe with a pro team or a college." The summer after completing his degree, he worked in two summer basketball camps, earning approximately $1,200. During the summer, he applied for three jobs in athletic administration at the following schools: Ohio State University, Keene State University, and Amherst College.

In each case, he received a form letter, which said, basically, "Thanks, but no thanks. We've had over 150 people apply for this position. We'll keep your résumé on file."

Eric was a bit discouraged but decided to try substitute teaching at a local high school. He did it twice and found he hated it. Over the next six months, he applied for approximately ten sports administration positions, including director of intramural sports, assistant athletic director, and assistant sports coordinator. He had one interview, but no job offer.

After being out of school for approximately fifteen months, he applied for a customer service position at The Travelers Insurance Company. During the interview, he was asked what he had been doing for the last year and what his career goals were. He didn't have clear and concise answers. In addition, the interviewer said, "Your résumé indicates you want a position in sports administration. Do you really want a job in customer service?"

Eric next applied for entry-level sales positions at two companies: a book publisher and a beer company. In each case, he was not interviewed. It's been two years since Eric completed his master's degree. He's only had a few interviews and no job offers. His confidence and motivation have dropped to an all-time low. What's aggravating this situation is that his two best friends have good jobs and like what they are doing. One is teaching at a high school in Connecticut, and the other is working as a management trainee at General Electric, earning approximately $48,000.

Assignment

Create three questions you will ask your classmates to discuss issues related to career management or significant points in this case study. What would you do next if you were Eric?

CASE STUDY—DUNNIA ULLOA

Coming to the United States from Ecuador at a young age was a life-changing event for Dunnia Ulloa. Learning the language and culture was both exciting and challenging. She explains:

> After I graduated from high school, my father was diagnosed with pancreatic cancer. My mother was his full-time helper and nurse. It was my responsibility to work and provide for the family. At this point, I realized I might not be able to attend college due to my family's financial status.

I decided to work full time and be a full-time student at Capital Community College (CCC) in Hartford, Connecticut. This was not easy, but it helped me become stronger and gave me confidence so that I could deal with whatever obstacles I faced.

A semester prior to graduating from CCC, my professor, Mary Jean Thornton, invited a group of Travelers representatives to our class. They discussed the opportunity to participate in a new internship program. I was encouraged by my professor to apply. I was accepted into the EDGE internship program before graduating CCC.

The internship was a great experience. My goal was to work hard and learn as much as I could. I was assigned two mentors, Kate Bolduc and Kate Conway, both strong women leaders well into their careers. They guided me with valuable advice, and most importantly they listened to what I had to say. This helped me envision who I wanted to become in the future.

I continued my education at Central Connecticut State University (CCSU) to attain my bachelor's degree in finance. At that time, I was still juggling two jobs and family responsibilities.

During my internship assignments at Travelers, I have met great individuals that I admire and look up to. I have also had the opportunity to travel, work on interesting projects, and attend workshops on interviewing, team management, and other workshops that gave me opportunities to meet other employees and interns.

After obtaining my finance degree at CCSU and graduating with honors, I was hired into the Financial Management Leadership Development Program at Travelers.

My advice to students is the following:

- ► Believe in yourself
- ► Take advantage of internships
- ► Find a mentor
- ► Work hard
- ► Break away from negative people and surround yourself by positive individuals
- ► Don't expect others to guide you in the right direction; it's your career and your responsibility to get to where you want to be
- ► Never give up

Assignment

Create three questions you will ask your classmates to discuss issues related to career management or specific issues related to this case study.

RESEARCH

BIBLIOGRAPHY

Dunn, G. "How to Reduce Workplace Stress." refresher.com website.

Hersey, P. and Blanchard, K. *Management of Organizational Behavior*. 4th ed. Englewood Cliffs, NJ: Prentice Hall, 1982.

Maxwell, J. C. "Getting Over Today's Success." injoy.com website.

McGregor, D. *The Human Side of Enterprise*. 1st ed. New York: McGraw-Hill Companies, 1960.

Phillips, K. "Performance Management: What Is It, Anyway?" HR.com website.

Thornton, P. B. *Be the Leader, Make the Difference*. 1st ed. Torrance, CA: Griffin Publishing Group, 2000.

Thornton, P. B. "Teamwork: Focus, Frame, Facilitate." Management Review (November 1992).

FURTHER READING

Beck, J. and Yeager, N. *The Leader's Window*, 1st ed. New York: John Wiley & Sons, Inc., 1994.

Brown, T. "How to Cut the Cost of Conflict." mgeneral.com website.

Colan, L. *Passionate Performance*. 1st ed. Dallas, TX: CornerStone Leadership Institute, 2004.

Gallwey, W. T. *The Inner Game of Work*. 1st ed. New York: Random House, 2000.

Handy, C. *21 Ideas for Managers*. 1st ed. San Francisco, CA: Jossey-Bass Inc., 2000.

Jones, L. *Jesus CEO: Using Ancient Wisdom for Visionary Leadership*. 1st ed. New York: Hyperion, 1995.

Kane, M. J. "CEO's Speak on Leadership, Integrity and Courage." The CEO Refresher website.

Kotter, J. *Leading Change*. 1st ed. Cambridge, MA: Harvard University Press, 1996.

Kouzes, J. and Posner, B. *The Leadership Challenge*. 2nd ed. San Francisco, CA: Jossey-Bass Publishers, 1995.

Krisco, K. *Leadership Your Way*. 1st ed. Alexandria, VA: Miles River Press, 1995.

Ouchi, W. *Theory Z: How American Business Can Meet the Japanese Challenge*. 1st ed. Reading, MA: Addison-Wesley, 1981.

Peters, T. *Re-imagine!* 1st ed. New York: Dorling Kindersley Publishing, 2003.

Pfeffer, J. and Sutton, R. I. "The Smart-Talk Trap." Harvard Business Review (May–June 1999).

Pritchett, P. *New Work Habits For A Radically Changing World*. 1st. ed. Dallas, Texas: Pritchett & Associates, Inc., 1994.

Schneider, D. M. and Goldwasser, C. "Be a Model Leader of Change." Management Review (March 1998).

Shechtman, M. *Working Without a Net*. 1st ed. New York: Pocket Books, 1994.

Stevens, M. *Extreme Management*. 1st ed. New York: Warner Books, 2001.

Tichy, Noel M., with Nancy Cardwell. *The Cycle of Leadership*. 1st ed. New York: HarperCollins Publishers, 2002.

Tichy, Noel M., with Eli Cohen. *The Leadership Engine*. 1st ed. New York: HarperCollins Publishers, 1997.

Verzuh, E. "Break it Down: A Guide to Project Management." businessthinkers.com website.

OTHER RESEARCH

Interviews and discussions were held with the following consultants, managers, and leaders:

Phil Beaudoin, Leadership Consultant, Managing Partner, Be the Leader Associates.

Ruth Branson, Senior Vice President, Human Resources, Shaw's Supermarkets.

Tricia Day, Chief Labor Relations Officer, Massachusetts Bay Transportation Authority.

Janice Deskus, Vice President, Training and Quality Implementation, CIGNA Health Care.

John Godfrey, Professor, Business Administration, Springfield Technical Community College.

Thomas A. Goodrow, former Vice President for Business and Economic Development, Springfield Technical Community College.

Brad Handy, Entrepreneur and College Instructor.

Michael Z. Kay, President and CEO, LSG Sky Chefs, Inc.

Dan Kelly, Vice President, Transportation Business, International Fuel Cells.

Ayn LaPlant, President and CEO, Beekley Corporation.

Sue Lewis, Executive Vice President and Chief Real Estate Officer, The Travelers.

John Nicoletta, Leadership Trainer, Managing Partner, Be the Leader Associates.

Mary Jean Thornton, College Professor, Former Executive, and Small Business Owner.

ABOUT THE AUTHOR

Paul B. Thornton is an author, speaker, trainer, and professor of business administration at Springfield Technical Community College in Springfield, MA. At the undergraduate level, he studied management, psychology, and political science at Ohio University. In addition, he earned an MBA degree from American International College and a Master of Education degree from Suffolk University.

He began playing organized hockey when he was twelve. By the time he entered Canton High School as a freshman, Paul had become good enough to make the varsity team. He was always curious to know why some teams in his league consistently excelled (unfortunately, that didn't include his team) and others floundered. Summoning all of his teenage wisdom, he concluded that the difference was due to coaching. Early on, he began studying what the top coaches did to bring out the best in their teams and in their individual players. This sparked Paul's lifelong interest in coaching, management, and leadership.

While a student at Ohio University, he took a terrific course taught by a terrific teacher: Managing Organizational Behavior by Dr. Paul Hersey. The knowledge and passion he gained from Dr. Hersey's class further ignited his interest in management and leadership. After graduating, no NHL teams were clamoring for his services. Paul worked a few years in sales, but that wasn't his passion. At age twenty-seven, he accepted a teaching and coaching position (varsity hockey) at American International College. This experience gave him the opportunity to apply some of the management concepts and leadership theories he had learned in college.

After teaching and coaching for five years, Paul accepted a position at the Hamilton Standard division of United Technologies. His initial job involved designing and conducting a variety of supervisory and management training programs. He rotated through several human resource functions, including recruiting, compensation, labor relations, and employee development.

Paul was promoted to leadership roles, including human resources manager for approximately 2,000 employees and manager-management training and development for approximately 300 managers and leaders. This position included conducting management assessment centers, designing and delivering management and leadership programs, and coordinating the company's succession planning and leadership development program. In 1985 and 1996, he was the recipient of a United Technologies Award for Extraordinary Management Effectiveness.

After Hamilton Standard, Paul and two friends started a management consulting company called "Be the Leader Associates." Paul has designed and conducted management and leadership programs for various companies, including Palmer Foundry, UMASS Medical School, Mercy Health Systems, Management Development International, Kuwait Oil Corporation, and United Technologies Corporation. Since 1980, he has trained over 20,000 supervisors and managers to be more effective leaders.

Paul has published articles in *The Leader-to-Leader Journal, Engineering Manager, Management Review, Leadership Excellence, Electronic Engineering Times, The Toastmaster, USA Today,* and *The CEO Refresher.* In addition, he is the author of thirteen books, which are available at amazon.com and bn.com. See below for the titles of some of his work:

- ▶ *Precise Leaders Get Results* has received numerous 5-star reviews on amazon.com.
- ▶ *Be the Leader, Make the Difference* was selected as "one of the best business books of all time" by *The CEO Refresher* website.
- ▶ *Leadership—Best Advice I Ever Got* was described by Marshall Goldsmith as containing some of the best coaching on leadership you will ever receive. In addition, it was recommended as one of the "Best Leadership Books Available" on leadingtoday.org.

Paul's email address is pthornton@stcc.edu.